Praise for *Your Story, Well Told*

"This book will help you to craft your memories with joy and art. Let Corey Rosen teach you how good-humored authentic story sharing, in any social and cultural context, beats those nasty public lying contests every time."

—Nancy Mellon, healing storyteller, counselor, and author of *Storytelling and the Art of Imagination* and *Healing Story*

"*Your Story, Well Told* by Corey Rosen is an invitation to enter the theater of living story with a ticket already in your hand. Drawing from his impressive background in film, improv, and radio, Corey uses key techniques and the unbridled enthusiasm of a skilled storytelling coach to discover, refine, and tell your life story to the applause of one or thousands. Everyone has a story—Corey's storytelling guide offers proven tips, exercises, and expertise to showcase yours."

—Kate Farrell, librarian, storyteller, and author of *Story Power*

"Corey Rosen's book is a great resource. I know I will return to it again and again for ideas, inspiration, and entertainment. It's like listening to a good story being told, while learning how to tell your own stories better."

—Samantha Harris, cohost of *Dancing with the Stars* and *Entertainment Tonight* and author of *Your Healthiest Healthy*

"I believe you should read this book cover to cover and trust in Corey as your storytelling coach because of his twenty-plus years of dedication to story mastery as a performer and a teacher. This book is his life's work. The greatest thing I believe Corey's book can do for you is to give you the confidence to believe your stories are worth developing and sharing. Maybe one day you'll be sitting in a theater, watching your story as a movie, or perhaps you'll be on stage, holding people in the palm of your hands with three stories you're unfolding in the petal structure. The key is to believe in yourself."

—Patrick Combs, writer, director, and star of *Man 1, Bank 0*

"Everyone is a storyteller; it's how we communicate, make friends, and go through life. But few of us would dare to tell a story in public for fear that it has to be a 'good' story. Corey's book demystifies everything. His book will help everyone have the confidence to share their story with the world. And the more we hear each other's stories, the better we'll understand each other. Get this book; give it to your kids and yourself."

—William Hall, cofounder of BATS Improv. and author/editor of *The Playbook: Improv Games for Performers*

Your Story, Well Told

Your Story, Well Told

Creative Strategies to Develop and Perform Stories That Wow an Audience

By Corey Rosen

mango
PUBLISHING

CORAL GABLES

Cover Design: Roberto Núñez
Cover Illustration: jongjawi/AdobeStock
Layout & Design: Roberto Núñez
Interior Illustrations: Bhairavi Kulkarni and Magnolia Rosen
Photo Credits: Jack and Jill Illustration by Bhairavi Kulkarni, Mind Map
Illustrations by Magnolia Rosen, Petal Structure Illustration by Magnolia
Rosen, Author Photo by Stu Maschwitz, Moth GrandSlam Photo by Kathleen
Sheffer, courtesy of The Moth, The Story Spine was created by Kenn Adams,
author of the book *How to Improvise a Full-Length Play: The Art of
Spontaneous Theater*.

For permission requests, please contact the publisher at:
Mango Publishing Group
2850 S Douglas Road, 2nd Floor
Coral Gables, FL 33134 USA
info@mango.bz

For special orders, quantity sales, course adoptions and corporate sales, please
email the publisher at sales@mango.bz. For trade and wholesale sales, please
contact Ingram Publisher Services at customer.service@ingramcontent.com or
+1.800.509.4887.

Your Story, Well Told!: Creative Strategies to Develop and Perform Stories that
Wow an Audience

Library of Congress Cataloging-in-Publication number: 2021930100
ISBN: (p) 978-1-64250-465-1 (e) 978-1-64250-466-8
BISAC category code SEL040000, SELF-HELP / Communication &
Social Skills

Printed in the United States of America

To Mom and Dad, my favorite storytellers.

Table of Contents

Foreword

This book is an excellent manual on storytelling, I assure you. The advice contained herein is exceptional. I'd like to share the story of why I said yes to writing the foreword and why I implore you to read it cover to cover and trust in Corey as a storytelling coach.

"Patrick, the lawyer who helped you is similar to Obi-Wan in *Star Wars*." It's night, and I, Corey, and our mutual friend Scott are standing in line outside a club in San Jose, California. We're waiting to see Alanis Morissette, a little-known artist Scott has recently discovered. *Jagged Little Pill* recently came out, and Alanis is still a good six months from attaining her stadium-packing status.

(Years later, in my book, *Cash Me If You Can*, I'll tell a story about Scott first playing "You Oughta Know" for me in his San Francisco apartment as it created an unforgettable memory, but that's another story for another time. Right now, I'm telling you a story of another moment that I've never forgotten.)

Corey and Scott worked together at "ILM," Industrial Light & Magic, the special effects home of George Lucas. I found it fascinating that ILM was in an old shopping mall, disguised to create the effect that there was "nothing special to see here." Inside, Corey and Scott had "holy-shit-amazing" jobs where they worked on *Star Wars* movies, which still held an untarnished legendary status.

In fact, Corey, Scott, and a guy named George worked at ILM, and George might have been out with us on this particular night as well.

Corey and George were roommates, but George has no role in this story other than to serve as a contrast to Corey. George always dressed in fashionable, expensive black clothes and wielded his job at ILM like a hood ornament on a Rolls Royce. In comparison, Corey always wore earth tones, and if I remember correctly (and as a storyteller, trust me, I usually do), Corey went to the Alanis show wearing a frumpy green, or maybe brown, corduroy jacket. Brown. I can see it now; Corey was in a brown corduroy coat and had on his signature round glasses.

Corey was enthusiastic, not snobbish, about his job working on one of the greatest stories ever told by one of the greatest storytellers of all time. The more I think about it, Corey should have wielded his Star Wars job like a Rolls Royce hood ornament because he was working at story mecca, but Corey was much too down-to-earth to do so. Life would later make it very clear to me that the best teachers are usually down-to-earth people who give freely and withhold nothing they know. That's what Corey has done in this book. He's written not to show off what makes him a great storyteller but rather to show you how you can become the same.

While Corey was at ILM, I was three years into my self-styled career as a motivational speaker, and my first book, *Major in Success*, had just been published. In stark contrast to Corey's job which was a conversation igniter at parties, my job was a conversation ender. "What do you do?" "I'm a motivational speaker." Thud. Suddenly, it seemed like I'd passed gas.

Anyway, as we wait under the yellow streetlights for entrance into the music venue, our sidewalk conversation turns to a recent real-life experience I'd had that everyone loved talking about—my recent high-profile escapade with a $95,000 junk-mail check. I'd deposited a phony check into my bank as a joke—the bank had accidentally cashed it—and I'd inadvertently gotten myself into what amounted to an insane series of events. In contrast to my occupation, everyone loved hearing about my gobsmacking banking experience.

The problem was, I didn't know how to tell my story well. It was too much story—six months of story arc, a dozen key characters, a bajillion plot twists—and I had too little storytelling knowledge to properly convey it. Well, that's not entirely fair because I'd already written the "narrative" out, all 25,000 words, and that version had gone viral on the internet before viral was a term. We'd say, "thousands upon thousands of people are reading it!" But it was just a "narrative," not yet a story. (Corey adeptly explains the critical difference between a narrative and a story in Chapter 2.)

Anyway, I was often prompted at social gatherings to tell my story. "Patrick cashed one of those fake checks you get in the mail, and it was for $95,000. Patrick, tell the story!"

With each failed attempt to convey the staggering experience I'd had in real life, I learned that "telling my story" was like playing Twister naked and alone for an audience. I was a story hack. No shame, we all have to start somewhere, but there's a particular pain that comes from turning story gold into story lead. I call it reverse alchemy. I desperately could have used this book you have in your hands. Corey has packed it with key concepts it took me years of failure to learn: story structures you can rely on such as Linear, Nonlinear, Petal, Bookend, Flashback, Hero's Journey, and much more. But I digress. I was failing as a storyteller.

Getting back to this particular night in the Bay Area, waiting to see Alanis scream about going down on her boyfriend in a movie theater, Corey says, "Patrick, your check story ought to be a movie because it perfectly matches the template of Joseph Campbell's Hero's Journey."

And there it is: twenty-two-year-old Corey, already a serious student of story, way back in 1995.

I believe you should read this book cover to cover and trust in Corey as your storytelling coach because of his twenty-plus years of dedication to story mastery as a performer and a teacher. This book is his life's work.

Here's the crazy part: 1995 is the last time I've seen Corey and the last time I talked to him. I moved to San Diego. We both lived our lives, raised kids, made a living at our chosen crafts, and zap, decades pass in a flash, it's twenty-five years later.

The reason I remember that night in front of the club so much is that Corey's words meant the world to me. His confidence in my story helped me believe it was worthy of developing. And so, I did, first into a one-man show that I toured around the world for fifteen years, then as a book, and, as I write this foreword, my story about the check is in production to be a Hollywood movie. Corey was right.

The greatest thing I believe Corey's book can do for you is to give you the confidence to believe your stories are worth developing and sharing. Maybe one day you'll be sitting in a theater watching your story as a movie, or perhaps you'll be on stage, holding people in the palm of your hand with three stories you're unfolding in the petal structure. The key is to believe in yourself.

And now you know the story of why, when Corey asked me to write this foreword, I said "absolutely." I wanted to help storytellers, novice and expert, know that Corey's book is a masterful guide to storytelling. I felt "You Oughta Know."

Patrick Combs, writer, director, and star of *Man 1, Bank 0* and author of *Major in Success, When You Are Bursting, Cash Me If You Can,* and
The Purpose Code.
San Diego, Oct 30, 2020

Introduction

Once upon a time, people gathered, regularly and irregularly, and shared their experiences and adventures as stories. Over campfires, mugs of ale, cups of tea, or at the side of their beds, they connected, laughed, cried, learned, and fell in love. Then, the world changed. It was gradual at first. Their villages became towns and cities. Their worlds closed. Their communication moved to phones, computers, emails, and text messages. But that didn't stop their experiences and adventures, nor their desire to share them. And despite technology's efforts to separate us, or to unite us through electronic means, people found ways still to connect. Communities assembled of friends and strangers alike—proving that we could share our knowledge, our pain, and our learnings in the best and most powerful way—the way our ancestors have for thousands of years—through storytelling.

I am writing this introduction during an unprecedented period of separation in our world—the rapid spread of COVID-19, an illness so deadly that most of the world is quarantined inside their homes, apartments, or shelters, while the brave medical community and people deemed essential-workers (such as postal and grocery professionals, that enable the rest of us stay supplied and nourished) steel themselves in the face of a very scary danger.

And yet, amidst the closed doors and social distancing, people are communicating more now than ever—on phones and FaceTime, group video calls and online performances. Storytelling is all around us, even when we are protected indoors.

And one day soon, when this is behind us, we will open our doors, and fill our theaters, cafes, and conference rooms once again, and tell our stories—the stories of what we did and who we were, before, during, and after this crisis.

This book is for everyone with a story to tell, whether you aspire to share that story on a stage, in a one-man show, to win a new client, or to your grandchildren on FaceTime. This book will help you develop your true stories from concept through performance. Using ideation techniques and methods from the world of improvisational theater, it teaches how to tease an idea along, using a variety of structures and editing approaches to bring out the inner life of any true story. Through brainstorming and development to performance and memorization techniques, I hope this book inspires you to get on a stage of any kind and tell your story.

Because a world with more stories is a world I want to live in.

Chapter 1

Why Storytelling

Friday 7:42 a.m. I got punched in the face in front of my daughter's school. By another kid's mom.

I drive my kids, Henry and Magnolia, to school every morning. It's a window of time I cherish; fifteen to twenty uninterrupted minutes together with my children, during which I can engage them in conversations about school, friends, and issues on their minds and can teach them things that matter to me.

I try to change it up so that we're not the dreaded family that stares at their phones as they drive.

And every day has a little different routine. For example, every Tuesday is "New Music Tuesday," where I curate a new (to them) playlist featuring a musical artist or genre with a short lesson.

Fridays are "Current Events," where we discuss topics like restorative justice and conflict resolution as it relates to them, such as discussing strategies to deal with bullying behavior at school. "Ignore them," was the advice I offered. "Bullies feed on your energy, and nothing takes away their power like ignoring them."

My ten-year-old daughter (now finishing fourth grade) keeps a journal, logging the start and end times for our daily drive. Over the span of three years, she kept this log every day, expanding the columns in her spiral bound notebook to include driver (Mom or Dad), total travel time, which sibling sat in the front seat (for fairness), as well as a "notes" column. "Notes" generally tracked unusual activity or special cases that may have affected our ride to school.

A particular highlight of our standard commute was the sighting of a specific father and son that waited for their bus on the corner of 26th and Castro Street. While some people may be seen on a regular basis, we took a particular liking to this pair, since the father was always on his phone, while the five-year-old child looked out and took in the world around him. "Dad/Son Corner" was the name of that particular spot, and a sighting elicited both a cheer in the car and a comment in Noli's "notes" column.

On other occasions, my car has broken down, I've forgotten (and gone back for) my bagel, and Henry's had a bloody nose. All were logged for posterity in her diary.

So, it's the last week of school, and we've left a few minutes past our normal departure time, at precisely 7:28 a.m.

The school they attend, Rooftop, is in the Twin Peaks neighborhood of San Francisco—one of the highest elevations in the city, beneath the iconic Sutro Tower. The final approach to school is a narrow, winding two-lane road in a residential district.

As I'm driving, I see a vehicle stopped in the opposite lane and a man standing on the right shoulder of the road. Sensing that he is waiting to cross the street, I slow to a stop to let him cross. While I am doing this, an aggressive jerk behind me, not seeing why I stopped, leans on their horn with a punishing blast.

I'm not a fan of road ragers. Tailgaters, honkers, and overly aggressive drivers push me to the opposite emotional state. They drive closer, or honk louder, I drive slower or act more cautiously rather than less.

So, ignoring the pest behind me, I assess the situation to be safe and roll forward. As I do, the vehicle on my tail keeps up the assault, honking and yelling. My reaction is to drive just as slowly and then to pull out "the move."

I did not invent "the move," and I'm surely not the only one I know that uses it. "The move" is where, when some irritating tailgater is closely following you, you step on the brake, forcing them to also brake. In its best usage, the tailgater gets the message and backs off. This motorist does not, and the honking and fury escalate.

They then proceed to a straight-up unsafe move in any situation—to overtake me, crossing the double-yellow line on this narrow, winding road, just a few blocks from an elementary school during the peak "drop off" rush hour.

It is precisely 7:42 a.m. (I know because it is logged in my daughter's diary) when I pull "the second move." I speed up.

As she attempts to, unsafely, overtake my car, I accelerate and close the gap as we reach the school's "drop off line." The angry driver is trapped in the oncoming traffic lane, with no room to merge back into the proper lane.

This is typically where most road rage encounters conclude. Drivers exchange middle fingers or colorful language and, feeling that they were in the right and the other person was not, go on their way and on with their day.

This is not how my day progresses.

I pull my orange Mini Cooper to the side of the road and let my daughter out. Before I can continue on to the middle school campus (to drop off my son), I see a woman stomping toward my car.

In front of dozens of parents, teachers, and crossing guards, she stops beside my open car window. My son in the passenger seat looks at me with concern as the woman screams, "You made me almost hit you!"

Breathing deeply in an effort to maintain my own composure in the face of a cursing, angry mother, I say, "Ma'am. I think you should take a deep breath and calm down."

Saying, "calm down" to an angry person is the worst thing I could have said. I see fire in her eyes. I have nowhere to run or move. In a plea for mercy, I improvise, "My child is in the car." Then it occurs to me—she is outside. I am inside! If I close the car window, the encounter will end! So, I reach for the switch, but before the window can close, her right jab catches me across the jaw and ear. "Ow!"

Throwing my car into first gear, I flee, leaving the woman standing in the road behind me, screaming obscenities, "That's right! Run away!"

Leaving wide-eyed bystanders all around, I accelerate forward to Henry's campus, abandoning the frenzy I've just created.

Pulling the car over to drop Henry off, he turns to me. "Why did that woman hit you, dad?" It occurs to me that I screwed up. Here I am, trying to model good behavior, but the aggressive jerk inside me revealed itself. "Well, I antagonized that woman by the way I drove. She shouldn't have honked at me, but I did the wrong thing."

And of all the lessons I've tried to teach my kids on our short drives to school, this may have been the most clear—watching their father do the wrong thing, antagonizing an angry person, and fueling a situation that led to physical violence.

"Maybe, you should have just ignored her?"

"Yup. I did the wrong thing."

On the last night of the school year, Noli updated her daily diary log in a Google Spreadsheet, graphing the travel-to-school data she collected all year. That morning's incident was logged, for posterity, and in all of our memories. May 27—arrival time 7:42 a.m. Notes: Dad Punched in Face.

Noli's Driving Log and Statistical Analysis

•••

The week after it happened, I told this story to my Uncle Ted and Aunt Marian while visiting their home in Los Angeles. The energy and immediacy of the story was still brimming, and the questions that followed were typical of those other people ask when I tell this story:

What happened next?

Did she get in trouble?

Are you ok?

My favorite reaction came from Uncle Ted, who calmly went into his house and returned with a very authentic-looking grenade. By the smirk on his face, I suspected it was a replica, though it appeared as real as you can imagine. He held it out to me. "Next time that happens, you should hold this on the window ledge while she's talking." He's kidding, of course. But it's perfectly in character for my uncle to hear a story and supplement it with his own witty insight.

This was followed by his own story, where he acquired the grenade—an actual "decommissioned" weapon he got as a "souvenir" after his military service and when he's used it in his lifetime. The story Uncle Ted shared with me was a story that connected me to him. My story triggered a memory for him that led to him telling ME a great story. That connection is what happened when I told you my story about getting punched in the face.

In short, my story did what stories are meant to do—I related something that happened to me. And in doing so, I opened a channel of communication so that Uncle Ted (and Aunt Marian, and my wife, and kids) could all reflect on their own incidents, stories, and experiences.

The author with Uncle Ted shortly after he pulled a fake grenade on him

•••

We all tell stories. All the time. It happens naturally every day. That's just what we do. If you have had that instinct to stand in a spotlight, on a stage, and to tell a story, you are already on your way. And while it might look easy, there's some craft going on.

Everyone does have a story. And a perspective. So, let's figure out what makes that story (YOUR story) great!

The Craft of Storytelling

While this is not intended to be a book about parenting, I will confess that I am a parent of school-aged children, so several of my stories explore these experiences, including the following:

I'm a huge Star Wars fan. When I was a kid, the movies activated my imagination and took me to a galaxy far, far away. As a kid growing up in the 1970s, I loved my Star Wars toys and the trading cards, and even dressed as my favorite characters with store-bought Halloween costumes.

When I graduated college, I was hired to work for the company that actually made *Star Wars*: George Lucas' visual effects company, Industrial Light & Magic. It was my pie-in-the-sky dream job. I was part of a crew tasked with digitally restoring the original 1970s movies for their 1990s "Special Edition" theatrical re-releases, and I also helped to create new characters and creatures for the "prequel" chapters that came out to great fanfare (though critical and fan disappointment) twenty-some years after the originals.

When I had my own child, Henry, I took particular pride in being able to share this interest with him—the next generation of Star Wars fans. He had his own toys, games, and his very favorite book as a two-year-old, *The Star Wars Action Figures Archive*. The book was a totally awesome catalog of every Star Wars action figure that had ever been made, organized by character.

Here is an excerpt of my son's loved nearly-to-death copy of this book.

Though he could not yet read, Henry and I would pore over this book and, by rote memorization, he would repeat back every name of the characters. "Boba FETT! Han SOLO! Admiral ACKBAR!"

Since he was a little bit too young to watch the films, the characters were weighted evenly in his young mind. Luke Skywalker had no more importance than Darth Vader, Imperial Officer, or Max Rebo (lead singer of the band that plays for Jabba the Hutt—nerd alert!).

As the holidays were approaching, I looked on eBay and found a huge lot of used Star Wars action figures for sale. Total score! I was getting so excited for him to discover his present and have his very own toys to play with.

Sorting through the package, I was not surprised to find them to be in mixed condition—while some were a little dirty or trampled, one was missing his entire head. One day while going through the book with my son, Henry lingered on the Bespin Security Guard. This was the one that had arrived headless.

I was torn. Should I include the broken, headless Bespin Security Guard along with the others in my child's Christmas offering? If I did, I'd better cover my tracks.

"You know, Henry," I offered, "sometimes, Bespin Security Guards don't have heads." Henry squinted, taking a final look at the picture, then shrugged his shoulders and turned the page. It really was amazing to watch his young mind imbibe this entire fantasy universe, just as I had at a young age.

Christmas Eve finally arrived, and, after supper, the kids were sent to bed to await Santa. Since our son was so young, rather than making him open all his presents, my wife and I created an elaborate toy "setup" of all the action figures for him to discover the next morning.

Our family's tradition is a bit odd—to signal to the kids that it's "ok" to come out of their room, we play possibly the most obscure Christmas Carol ever written: "Dominic The Donkey," a jaunty tarantella about a Sicilian Donkey.

Timed with the song's opening accordion chords, the gates were opened and the children released unto the booty awaiting them. Henry raced to the mantle and, mouth wide open, locked his eyes on the action figures from his book, in real life! He jumped up and down as the carefully positioned characters tumbled over. I furiously photographed his jubilant discovery.

Crouching down, Henry examined the characters, experiencing, for the first time, objects he had only before seen as photographs in a book. "I got Max Rebo!"

"Great!!"

"I got Darth Vader!"

"Awesome!"

And then, he stopped in his tracks. "Dad! Dad! I got a Bespin Security Guard Without a Head!!!"

A tear rolled down my cheek. "Yeah. Awesome!"

That toy has since become one of our all-time favorites. The headless secondary character, who lived a fuller life in the imagination of a child and his father than anyone could have imagined, in this galaxy or another, far, far away.

Sometimes, Bespin Security Guards don't have heads.

While not a perfect example, let's take a look at that story.

The objects we collect or surround ourselves with are only as valuable as we allow them to be. Here was a broken toy, a damaged object which I could have thrown away. But by changing its narrative, I changed its fate. Bespin Security Guard, as equally important a character to my son as any other, could be headless and no less amazing.

The "craft" of storytelling allows us to take a moment, like my son opening his Christmas presents, and give it a bigger meaning. Something more fundamentally appealing and universally relatable.

I could have told that story in a much simpler way, sure, without the elaborate backstory. I could have simply written: I gave my son a lot of Star Wars figures for Christmas one year and one of them was broken, but he liked it, anyway.

Would that have carried the same feeling? The same emotion? Anything that might last or stand out in your mind in a day, a week, a month? I think not. Storytelling imbues an experience or memory with context, character, and feeling which gives that simple action of "gifting a kid a broken toy for Christmas" a larger purpose. And hopefully, the kind of feeling that might create an empathetic response or memory from the person hearing it. It's this effect that makes a story elevate beyond itself. It creates a connection between the teller and the listener or reader. The story becomes not just my experience. It has the opportunity to become a connector of people's lives and experiences (at best) or a pleasant (or emotionally resonant) distraction at worst.

This is a very different type and scale of story from my Getting Punched in the Face story. Each has its own social and cultural subtexts. The first speaks to a greater degree of the times we live in; dads ignoring their children while on their cell phones, and neighbors dramatically assaulting each other over perceived slights… The second has less social commentary, as a personal story about creating meaning between a parent and their child.

I think the Bespin Security Guard story is "cute existentialism." It's a story without meaning—and where meaning is created. A toy arrives broken that could be discarded, or that could be an opportunity for a story, a story that creates a larger meaning. A broken toy turns a negative situation to a positive one, and a personal connection between a father and a son. A story, in other words, about storytelling itself. How a story can change a situation and a person's view or perception of the world around and in front of them.

When many of my students begin a storytelling class, they often come in with a sense of "I have so many great stories, I just need a forum to tell them—I'm ready for my one-woman show!" When they start telling them, it is clear that they have lived interesting lives with varied and notable experiences. What also frequently becomes clear is that the stories are raw, rough, difficult to track, and lacking in a cohesive learning or change-inducing moment. In short, unpracticed or worked stories fail to feel like stories at all—they sound like related memories.

What's the difference?

Memories sound episodic, isolated, and without meaning. They are things that happened to you, or to people in your life, or to a group that you were a part of. They feel, in your memory, important because you remember that feeling when you lived it—of surprise, shock, pain, love, loss, etc. But when you convey them to your friends (or classmates), without the context and perspective, those kinds of stories tend to fail.

On the contrary, listening to a story can be a transformative experience—an interruption that can have a profound effect on your life. Listening to a story allows us to, in the much-more-academic words of Nathaniel Dorsky in his lecture on *Devotional Cinema*, "subvert our absorption in the temporal and reveal the depths of our own reality. It opens us to a fuller sense of ourselves and our world."

This reminds me of the feeling I get after I watch a story told to me live. I lose myself through the telling, absorbed in the experience of hearing the person's experience, and reflect back on myself and my own.

That's what I want out of my stories, don't you?

Let's look again at my "punched in the face" story. This story happened to me—but also in front of my children who witnessed it and formed their own memories, emotions, and conclusions based on it.

Here is a verbatim transcription of the way my son Henry tells the story of what happened that morning (when conveying it to a mutual friend).

> So, we were like a week from when school was gonna be over. And we were driving to school, like, normally. So, we're like a block away from school and my dad's driving and there's some guy trying to get into his car on the street and on the other side there's like a big truck coming. So, my dad is, like, waiting for the guy to get into his car. But there's a person behind him and they're really close.
>
> So, my dad does kind of a jerky thing where he steps on the brakes. He steps on them fast. That made the person really mad. They tried to go around my dad so then my dad does the second jerk thing. He speeds up. Now the person is in oncoming traffic and my dad is going to school.
>
> So, my dad pulls over and Noli gets out of the car and we see an angry lady walking down the street. And then my dad rolls down the window. "You can't slam on the brakes like that! You

can't do that!" I'm sitting in the front seat and I knew this was the person that was on the street and they start yelling at my dad. And my dad says, "Ok, I think you have road rage. Take a deep breath." And then she's just really mad, "don't tell me to take a deep breath." And I was scared because I didn't know what she was gonna do.

So, then my dad's like, "I have children in the car." And she says, "I have children, too!" This is a mom from our school. And this is all happening as drop-off is happening. The principal is down there. There are school busses all around. And there's parents dropping their kids off, and there are teachers... Everybody is seeing this.

So then, she reaches through the window and punches my dad! But my dad kind of dodges it, so it hits the back of his head. But she threw a punch at my dad.

So, at that point, my dad is driving away, and then she's like, "are you running over my toe?" She's in the middle of the street and she's swearing, saying a lot of bad words. And then we just drove away. And that person turns out to be a kid in my class's mom. So that was pretty crazy. But luckily, I wasn't late to school.

Do you notice the similarities and differences between these two remembered versions of the same incident? Places where the storyteller(s) included or excluded information? Nearly every aspect of the stories, aside from the climactic action of the punch, is different!

The structure—where we begin and end—is different.

In my version, I start and end with the routine of our day. My children's routine of writing the times we leave for and arrive at school and interesting incidents that happen along the way. *That morning's incident was logged, for posterity, and in all of our memories. May 27—arrival time 7:42 a.m. Notes: Dad Punched in Face.*

In Henry's version of the same story, he pretty much jumps right into the action of the story. *"So, we're like a block away from school and my dad's driving and there's some guy trying to get into his car."* He also ends the story from his own perspective, *"Luckily, I wasn't late to school."*

The dialogue between the characters is slightly different:

In my version of the story, I recalled the woman saying, *"You almost made me hit you!"*

Henry's recollected telling of the story presents the dialogue as, *"You can't slam on the brakes like that! You can't do that!"*

And the conclusions—how or if the story wraps up and terminates— varies widely from storyteller to storyteller.

The point I am making here is not to mock my elementary and middle school aged children's abilities as storytellers, but to stress with one example how and why the action of telling, working, editing, reworking, and performing a story can and will make it better, stronger, more effective, and more impactful over time.

Some people may actually prefer Henry's version of the story! It's raw. It's real. It's a kid's perspective.

Through this book this is what we will home in on, with opportunities for you to insert and work on your own stories and storytelling.

The Business of Storytelling

Stories are persuasive. They can mean the difference between buying this product or another one. Hiring one vendor over another one. Promoting one employee over another.

Many people's businesses involve them standing up in front of a group of people, giving presentations and maybe using charts, tables, or graphics.

Whether in school or at work, most of us have been on the "receiving" end for this kind of presentation. Think about ones that stood out, that succeeded in changing your opinion or your mind.

What did that person do differently or better than an ordinary "salesman"?

Was it the quality of their graphics? Perhaps that helped.

I believe the best way to turn a bad presentation into a good (or great) presentation is through storytelling. If a story can connect two friends, it can certainly do more to connect two strangers or business associates than a spreadsheet or graph shown in PowerPoint.

Our brains won't retain data or facts told to us without an emotional connection to them, which is what stories do. Stories put faces and feelings to experiences and the result is a connection between those people.

When Henry ran for Student Council treasurer, he had to give a short speech to the entire school. All the other kids listed their campaign "promises."

> "If I'm elected, you'll get a longer RECESS!"
>
> "If you vote for me, I'll make the school put a fan in every classroom!"
>
> "Vote for me and we'll have pizza parties every Friday!"

I encouraged him to tell a story instead. This is what he wrote:

On the first day of first grade, I got lost and I got confused of where to go. The only person and the only class I knew was Ms. Cruz's kindergarten because that's what I knew from before. I wandered down to Ms. Cruz's class, and Ms. Cruz took me into her classroom, put me on the couch, and I fell asleep. I learned that day that Rooftop is a place where people take care of each other.

I've come a long way since kindergarten and first grade. Now I know Rooftop like the back of my hand. I've been here my whole academic life, and I want to give back to Rooftop because I've gotten so much from it. I am Henry Rosen, and I am running for treasurer of the student council.

•••

In retelling this story, I'm reminded of the power of a story in any kind of sales situation. And, oh yes, this was a sales situation. Anytime someone tells you a story that makes you change your mind or your behavior, you are being sold something.

Not that my son was trying to manipulate anyone in that story, but he certainly was selling something—himself.

And from that experience, he closed the sale. People voted for him and he won the election.

He shared a personal memory where he was vulnerable and scared, emotions felt by most, if not all, the other kids in his class. And he learned a lesson that he could reflect on and project forward that connected to the product he was selling: his commitment to his school and his desire to give back by serving them on Student Council.

He won because he gave them what they wanted. A good story is not just an interesting series of events—it's something that, when told, creates or illuminates meaning for someone else's life. "Henry loves this school. I love this school too, and I want someone like him to represent me."

Everywhere you look nowadays, you are being told a story. Stories are in the ads on your train commuting to work, the ads on your radio as you drive, and in the classrooms you, your friends, or your children are attending.

Beyond the field of "entertainment," it's increasingly clear that the path to effective communication in business, dating, and more is through story. Learning and applying the skills contained here can help in myriad ways.

The tools and analyses I put on my own stories with these past few pages are what I will have you do as we go forward. To introduce the tools so you too can look at, analyze, and hone the meaning of your own stories. Transcend your own meanings, and share your stories.

The Fun of Storytelling

This is a game I play in my classes—often on the first day of class. It's called "That Reminds Me of the Time."

With a partner and working from a prompt suggested by the group leader (or one of the participants), each partner relates a single simple, condensed memory fragment inspired by that prompt.

> Example: for the prompt "cheese"—Cheese reminds me of ordering a Domino's pizza to be delivered to a Chinese restaurant when I was a kid (a true story).

Without elaborating any more on that story, the other partner says "That reminds me of that time…" with a memory in some way connected to the last memory.

> Example: That reminds me of the time my family went to a Chinese restaurant for my uncle's birthday dinner.

The connection should be relatively clear (e.g. Chinese Restaurants). It doesn't have to be the most interesting story in the world. It doesn't have to relate to the entire memory of the last person. And it definitely doesn't have to be explained or elaborated on.

Go back and forth.

> Uncles… That reminds me of the time my uncle took me to a horse track for the first time.
>
> Horse Track… That reminds me of this rodeo I went to while driving across the USA.
>
> Road trips… That reminds me of a fight I had with my ex while on a road trip.
>
> Fights… That reminds me of this restaurant I was in when I finally broke up with my girlfriend.
>
> Etc.

A good "rule" is that each memory should "stand alone" in a way by adding some unique information that the other partner can use to inspire their memory. Less helpful is "That reminds me of the same thing that happened to me!" If the "same thing" did happen to you, be specific about it:

> That reminds me my girlfriend dumped me in a sushi restaurant—the kind with the boats that go around and around.

Adding some other detail can help the game continue and not stall out. That last prompt can steer a sushi memory. Or a boating memory. Or a restaurant memory.

This kind of "ideation" exercise can, in a rapid and often hilarious manner, rattle some rather surprising and "hidden" story material from your life!

Definitely a fun game to play for anyone who says, "I don't have any good stories." We all are full of memories, experiences, and relationships, any of which can, with the right tools, be developed from a "good idea" or "something that happened" to the world of "a good story."

The difference, as we've already explored, is in the telling and the developing of that story. "Getting dumped in a sushi restaurant—the kind with the boats that go around and around" is not a story—yet...

If the idea of developing one of these memories or ideas into a story seems like "work," there is a simple initial remedy—tell someone else your story.

All my students who say "I didn't work on my story this week" between classes, or "I don't have a story to tell" in class will, without exception, remember a story in the course of the evening. Or in retelling a past story, find themselves remembering and reconnecting with the emotion and detail of having lived that experience.

At a recent Berkeley *Moth StorySLAM*, a man was selected to come up to tell his story. The topic for the audience was "Confessions." He had put his name in "the hat" on a whim, thinking he would not be picked. When he was, he grabbed the attention of the audience immediately with a confession, "I've never told this story to anyone in my entire life. And tonight, I am here with my two daughters, one of their boyfriends, and his mother."

The stakes were already enormously high, and we didn't have any idea what we were about to hear. The man's apparent terror at what he was about to "confess" along with his seemingly giddy delight at finally getting it off his chest in a four-hundred-person, sold-out theater of strangers and the closest people in his life, made the entire building "lean in" for the ride he was about to take us on. (More about that story in Chapter 8.)

When we retell our true stories, there is no work to do at all. We are harnessing the fun, pain, or whatever specific emotion that story brings out in us as we reflect on the experiences that shaped us. Bringing meaning to these experiences through retelling them connects us to the people around us, friends and strangers alike.

Exercise: That Reminds Me of the Time

Try this, by yourself or with a friend—out loud or on paper.

Start with a word: _____

That reminds me of the time: _____

_____

_____

_____

That reminds me of the time: _____

_____

_____

_____

That reminds me of the time: _____

_____

_____

_____

That reminds me of the time: _____

_____

_____

_____

That reminds me of the time: _____

_____

_____

_____

That reminds me of the time: _____

_____

_____

_____

That reminds me of the time: _____

_____

_____

_____

That reminds me of the time: _____

_____

_____

_____

That reminds me of the time: _____

_____

_____

_____

That reminds me of the time: _____

_____

_____

_____

That reminds me of the time: _____

_____

_____

_____

That reminds me of the time: _____

_____

_____

_____

That reminds me of the time: _____

_____

_____

_____

Chapter 2

What Is a Story?

How Do We Define a Story?

sto·ry[1] stôrē/ *Noun*

1. *An account of imaginary or real people and events told for entertainment. Synonyms: tale, narrative, account, anecdote.*

2. *An account of past events in someone's life or in the evolution of something. "The story of modern farming."*

Ok. But what's a STORY (really)? Is it just the accounting of an event and people for entertainment? Of course not. Relating an account of "what happened" in someone's life of the evolution of something might be defined as a story, but it sure doesn't feel like one.

When my son, Henry, recollected the events on the day his dad was punched in the face in Chapter 1, he's not telling us a story. He's recollecting a memory without meaning or perspective. He's relating

---

1   (Source: dictionary.com)

it as one would to their inherited audience: your family, close friends, etc. People in our inherited audience get a pass when they relate these memories. They're in the tribe. We give them credit and fill in the gaps. We put some of our own meaning onto their stories and draw connections that don't work when the circle expands.

When Henry told his version of what happened that day, it was an expression—not a story. And in my mind, it's perfect. It's what a twelve-year-old felt about an incident he witnessed, just as an adult may relate an event as they witnessed it to their best friend. It's engaging, and it's as detailed as it needs to be to function as their impression of the incident…but it's not a story, not yet!

You don't have a story until you've made it a story. Similar to how someone who is funny is often told, "you should do stand-up!" Stand-up, like storytelling, is a craft.

A story differentiates something that "happened" in one very important way—something or someone changed because of it. Or was changed in light of it. In a dramatic or subtle way, the world was altered after the events described in "what happened." This could be an inward change (I never looked at her the same way again). This could be an outward change (I quit the job, changed careers, and never looked back). This change could affect your private world (I know my daughter is growing up). Or this change could affect the planet (Thanks to this discovery, 60,000 people are now being delivered clean water per day).

Getting from "the idea" to "the story" is not always clear. What we think of as "the story" might be the dictionary definition of a story (accounting the events as you remember them).

Here are some other writers' definitions of what storytelling is all about:

*"A Story is a chain of events that...seems to begin
at one place and to end at a very different place,
without any essential interruption in its progress."*

—RANDALL JARRELL (*RANDALL JARRELL'S BOOK OF STORIES: AN ANTHOLOGY*)

"A tale shall accomplish something and arrive somewhere."

—MARK TWAIN (*THE MARK TWAIN COLLECTION: HIS NOVELS,
SHORT STORIES, SPEECHES, AND LETTERS*)

A "narrative" describes what happened. A "story" is told for a reason, taking a narrative's sequence of events to a higher level that can reveal or reflect on that sequence's significance.

What Do Stories Have in Common?

Let's look at some story examples we've already explored to see what they have in common:

- The Punch in the Face Story
- The Broken *Star Wars* Toy Story
- The Student Council Election Story

Characters:

- All of these stories feature distinctive characters

    - The angry driver

    - The *Star Wars*-loving child

    - The scared first grader

- All of these stories also include peripheral characters:

  - The onlookers, school administrators, and other children

  - The eBay auction seller

  - Ms. Cruz, the kindergarten teacher

Conflict:

- Inward forces of conflict:

  - Am I teaching by example?

  - Do I lie to my own child?

  - Am I lost?

- Outward forces of conflict:

  - Road rage leading to physical violence

  - "Buyer Beware" perils of purchasing used/damaged goods

  - All the rooms in the school look the same

Change:

- Inward Change:

  - I learned not to antagonize a bully

  - An object's value is completely subjective

  - I felt taken care of by my community

- Outward Change:

  - My behavior changed because of something my son taught me

  - A child can derive pleasure from their own imagination

  - I can give back to my community

But what is a "Good Story?"

Just having characters, conflict, and change doesn't necessarily make a story "good," does it?

Any of the previous example stories could be told with the characters, conflict, and change in a way that would not be "good" storytelling.

This is my version of "bad" storytelling:

My school's drop off area is on a narrow street. A woman was tailgating me one time, beeping her horn. She tried to get around me, but I sped up which made her really mad. She punched me in the face!

That had my three ingredients, but it's missing a lot.

"Good" storytelling can seem a tricky thing to pin down, but it's not simply a matter of "I'll know it when I hear it."

To paraphrase Robert McKee from his masterpiece, *Story,* a "good story" is nothing unless it is "well told."

Characters:

- The harried parents rushing kids off to school who lose their cool

- A parent covering his own tracks with an invented detail to a trusting child

- A lost child wandering through the halls of an unfamiliar school

Conflicts:

- I have felt mad behind the wheel of my car too

- I feel the need to lie to manage expectations on Christmas morning

- I have felt scared and lost

Changes:

- A perspective-shift illustrated by this experience

- I can be a real jerk behind the wheel of the car

- Creativity can be more valuable than money

- The school took care of me. I want to take care of it.

As a story develops from its "narrative" nascent state, these elements can be laced in, embellished, and modified to suit the flow of the story. In applying them, like spices in a recipe, your narrative experiences take shape and elevate beyond what happened into a fuller and richer experience worth sharing.

How do I know if I have a "good story?"

There's a practical way to gauge if you have a good story. Tell it to someone. Do they like it? If so, what do they like about it?

The standout parts of your story will make your audience lean in, smile, nod, and cry. The parts they do not connect with will have the opposite effect—they will look away, think about something else, blink their eyes, tilt their head with confusion, and not laugh at the parts you think are funny.

Storytelling is a skill best practiced by telling stories. Audiences, whether by phone or in person, numbering one or a thousand, are the best indicators of how and where your stories work and struggle.

As we will explore in the next chapter, it's important to tell your stories in all phases, even when they are raw and developing. It is through these reactions that your most sincere and authentic feedback is received. It is from these trials that the real fun/work can begin.

Here is a story I will refer to a few times throughout this book. It's included here verbatim as I performed it at *The Moth*, and as it appeared on *The Moth Radio Hour*. I've kept all my awkward sounding "likes" and all to give a sense of how this sounded on stage, live—without cleaned-up, nuanced grammar fixing. I'm tempted to clean it up—to add literary craft to the written version of the story—but I realize that I want to present, as true as I can, the audio version of this story.

That's my disclaimer. Here's the Cousin Norman story, called "The Secret":

My story tonight is about my cousin Norman. Norman Weiner. That's his real name.

Norman died. He died in August, August 1. He died at the age of eighty-two. It was unexpected. Even though he was eighty-two. He wasn't sick. He wasn't dying. He didn't know he was going to die. It wasn't one of those "you've been sick for a long time" cases. It was just, like, he had this lump, and he went to get it checked out. It was kind of a routine thing. The doctors decided we'll take the lump out. They took the lump out! The lump was fine, but the hole made an infection and the infection made pneumonia and pneumonia made no more Norman.

Which is really sad because I was pretty close with Norman and being sort of the designated person in my family on the West Coast, I was their representative. Most of my family is back East. They kind of designated that I was going to be the guy to tie up the loose ends. I was going to go his apartment, kind of go through his things. What was the stuff we were going to keep? And what was the stuff we were going to get rid of or salvage? That kind of thing...

And that's when I discovered Norman had a secret.

So, let me tell you a little bit about Norman first. Norman was a real character. Norman was very tall which was a huge anomaly in my family. We're all normal, Jewish, height, sort of the five foot eight, five foot nine cut off. Norman was like six and a half feet. He had giant glasses and giant ears and a giant nose.

He would tell these stories. "Oh Corey, I gotta tell you about this wonderful movie that I saw. It was called *Seven*, but it was so dark. Corey it was dark, dark. This is a dark movie! When the movie was over, I was looking for my sunglasses. I had my sunglasses on Corey!"

Norman was a teacher who spent his life teaching English in high schools. He never married. He never had a partner in his life. So, he traveled all by himself. He used the teacher's schedule and would go on these long summer trips.

He was a frugal guy. You know, he saved his pennies. He'd go on, like, those Atlantic crossing transition/repositioning cruises. You know what I'm talking about—sort of cheap—and he'd stay in the hostels with the backpackers even though he was, like, an old guy, because he didn't care. He didn't care.

He loved theater. He loved opera. He loved the arts and he just took it in, and he didn't care about comforts. You know, like staying on the concierge level at the Marriott. He didn't care about those things. He cared more about seeing things, you know, like getting experiences.

But my whole family, like a lot of people in my family, all thought of him...they talked shit about Cousin Norman. They would say he was frugal. They would say he's a cheapskate. They would talk down about these decisions that he made in his life, which I thought was terrible. Because I love the guy.

He would regale us with these stories, because he REALLY loved theater. You know he would say, "Oh, I saw Lawrence Olivier, Corey! I was at the Old Vic and he was Hamlet. Oh, it was great!" And he remembered everything!

So, I did a show about ten years ago called *The A**hole Monologues*. It was a charity for Crohn's disease, which affects assholes, and he's like, "I want to write an a**hole monologue Corey about Shakespeare's assholes! There's so many! Richard the Third: what an ass-HOLE!" He wrote, and he performed this thing. It was fantastic and I loved it.

And my son's birthday—he shared it with Norman. They were one day apart. So, when my son Henry turned one, we had a first and eightieth birthday celebration together. It was awesome. He took the train up—it was the cheapest way to come up from Long Beach—and he slept in our guestroom and it was really wonderful. It was one of the last times that I saw Norman.

So, I'm in his apartment, by myself. Like, I let myself in, and I'm cleaning out his apartment and I have that weird moment you know when, like, you're...I don't know if any of you have ever had to do this thing. It was my first time where you're there, clearing out the stuff and deciding what to keep what to lose and I'm like "where's the secrets?"

You know I'm sad but I'm also, like, alone in somebody's stuff and it's making me think about what it would be like in my *own* house. Like, when I go, what's the weird narrative that people are going to put together when they see *my* shit, and my four hundred snow globes and my box of random pictures and that little tiny bag of hash in the freezer?

All those things that you just have and how you think that are important. "That's not important."

And the experience was really overwhelming.

And so, I packed up the car. I did it. I skipped my flight that was supposed to fly home, but I just packed up this rental car. I drove all the way home at dawn. I spent like twenty hours in his apartment, clearing out the stuff and when I got home, I looked through all these carousels of pictures that he'd taken.

He traveled to dozens of countries. He had passports, ten passports, filled with visas and stamps and all this stuff. And I got to see his life through his pictures—through his eyes, the trips that he took. It was so overwhelming to see. And they weren't, like, pictures of him in front of stuff. It was just, like, what *he* saw. They were *bad* pictures. You know, like, the pictures that people take when you get off the tour bus. It was really emotional.

And then I read the will. And that's where the secret was. Because it turns out that Norman was loaded. And that I was in the will. And all my *fucking* family, who had written off Cousin Norman, the cheapskate, the frugal cheapskate, who were never nice to Norman... And I didn't want anything from Norman.

I just loved him. I loved who he was and how he was. And Norman didn't want to die. He didn't plan to die. He had enough money for twenty years of luxury travel, but he was saving it. And he gave it—he gave it to my family. And now my kids can go to college. And I miss him.

Story Structures

In a discussion of "story structure" it is important to clarify my philosophy and approach to the subject, which is that there is no single structure that is applicable to all stories. Every story deserves and often demands its own approach and method by which it would work best.

Think of some of your favorite books, plays, or movies. More than think of, examine them and break down their inner machinations, their inner structures. Break them apart to see what those writers, creators, and storytellers are doing to make effective stories work.

My friend and colleague Seth Worley developed an excellent diagnostic tool for just this purpose called the Story Notebook. With this handy reference tool, you can note the key moments in a story as they transpire, for analysis later of the patterns that lie within— what is a setup and payoff? How are multiple storylines introduced, developed, woven in and around others, and ultimately resolved?

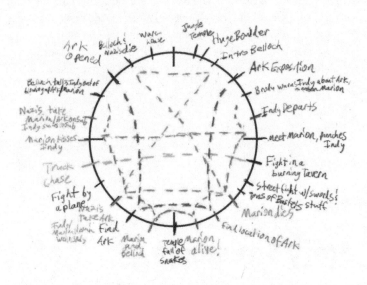

Raiders of the Lost Ark mapped using the Story Clock (courtesy of PlotDevices.co)

In this section, I will introduce a few different story structures. By doing so, I aim to illustrate how they can be used as both creation aides as well as diagnostic resources to edit and strengthen your stories.

Linear Stories

The basic building block of storytelling is the "Linear Story." This is, as it sounds, when a story unfolds in a linear, chronological order. This happens. Then, this happens. Then, something else happens.

Teacher, storyteller, and improviser Kenn Adams succinctly captured the basic linear story structure into a tool used the world over, *Kenn Adams' Story Spine*.

Kenn Adams' Story Spine uses eight to nine simple "starter" phrases to grab the essence of what, who, how, and why the narrative in a story transpires. Here it is:

Once Upon a Time...

And Every Day...

Until One Day...

And Because of That...

And Because of That...

And Because of That...

Until Finally...

And Ever Since That Day...

(Optional) The Moral of the Story is...

Let's take a little deeper dive into this to explore just what's happening in the Story Spine and how it can be used.

Once Upon a Time

Whether these words are literally said in a story or not, every story contains the essence of "Once Upon a Time." It can mean, generally:

- Who the story is about?
  - Once upon a time, there was a farm girl

- Where the story takes place
  - Once upon a time, there was a farm girl who lived in Kansas

- The general world of the story

  - Once upon a time, there was a fish who lived in a coral reef off the coast of Australia

- The time of the story

  - Once upon a time, there was a farm boy who lived on a desert planet called Tatooine

"Once Upon a Time" is a critically important component of your story. If we, the audience, do not know what your "world" is, we will be confused. Confusion is not necessarily a bad thing—it can be used deftly to create suspense and intrigue if the audience is being intentionally held back from knowing certain information. But if that information never comes—and the audience is left in the dark (unintentionally), you will lose our attention.

Understanding the "Once Upon a Time" of your story, whether that is a seventh-grade girls' bathroom, a church basement in the 1990s, or the top of a ladder in a multi-million-dollar home creates a comprehension for the listener about the situation, the location, and the setting in which the story takes place.

Here is the beginning of a story I tell:

> I'm holding two buttons. In my right hand, the button controls the television. In the left, the button controls my morphine drip. I'm twenty years old, recovering from a near fatal car accident at Rochester General Hospital.

While I didn't use the words "Once Upon a Time" or even start with the setting, in short order, the story grabs the attention and curiosity of the listener (I'm holding two buttons. "Two buttons? Why? What do the buttons do?") and then satisfy their curiosity with the setting, time, and place (the hospital, when I was younger). There are still a lot of unanswered questions, as well as some setup for key elements that will play into the story later (the morphine, specifically), but the "Once Upon a Time" creates, with these few lines, a context for the story that is starting to unfold.

A metaphor I enjoy using is that of a blank canvas. Imagine as you, the storyteller, start to speak, that you are filling in a blank canvas in the mind of the listener. They see and imagine nothing that you do not add to that canvas. With the paint and brushes that you choose, and when you choose to do so, you fill in the canvas with details, narrative, and colors that create, in the end, a complete picture of your experience.

By setting the "Once Upon a Time" for the listener, you are giving them more than the context for the story that you are telling them— you are calibrating expectations. You are initiating what Keith Johnstone terms a "circle of probability" for what behaviors are expected, allowed, and encouraged in this environment.

This can, of course, be used to set up your audience for reversals of expectation, or to pay off assumptions and understandings that they carry with them about that experience.

Generally speaking, every story starts out with a very large circle of probability. As new information is shared, that circle shrinks. In a hospital, we generally understand the "rules" of how things operate, how and who might come into the room periodically, and what one may or may not be wearing. You would not expect a spaceship to land, or a bear to speak in this story, the way I have set it up.

In the *Finding Nemo* example, by contrast, by setting a world where fish can speak, emote, and behave as a community might, we have other calibrated understanding and expectations—such as that they generally behave as fish—unable to breathe out of the water, unable to communicate directly with humans, unable to walk on two feet, etc.—even if we are able to "hear" them through the special magic that is animation.

In a true story, the circle of probability can expand, rather can contract, when a pattern or routine of any kind—itself suggesting a circle of probability—is broken or disrupted, such as when the routine of waking up in the morning is disrupted by finding you are in the wrong bed. Or the wrong apartment. Still, we the audience will recalibrate to this situation, and subsequent actions will clarify and shrink the circle of probability, expecting logical actions and behaviors to occur within its confines.

And Every Day

The second stanza in the Kenn Adams' Story Spine, "And Every Day…" fulfills another specific duty in the service of a story—defining what is "normal."

We all live our own lives, ordinary or extraordinary. What is commonplace for the child of a parent struggling with morphine addiction may be very different from the "every day" of a wealthy suburbanite. Luke Skywalker's "every day" dream of running away from his boring life as a moisture farmer on Tatooine can also be, by contrast, quite similar to Dorothy Gale's "every day" dream of running away from her boring life on a Kansas farm to a place "over the rainbow."

What is crucial, for the story to succeed in drawing us in, with empathy and understanding, is to name the "everyday" for you, your situation (as it relates to this narrative), and the world as it currently exists.

By using (or not using) the words "and every day," this does not need to imply that "everyday" is in balance. Many people's life situation can be "normal" in a state of unrest or ill at ease.

- And every day, I longed to find the mother that gave me up for adoption

- And every day, I walked the same route to and from my downtown Chicago apartment building

- And every day, I waited by the mail hut for news from the other side of the world

"And Every Day" for my hospital story might sound something like:

- And every day, I languished in bed, recovering from the physical and emotional stresses of having survived my terrifying collision with a tree on the side of a California Highway just days earlier

In addition, "And Every Day" serves a critical narrative purpose in the story spine—the creation of a pattern. While we are not you, and we have not lived your life, we understand the routines and patterns of a person's life. If you set up a pattern for us, we will understand your "normal" world. This communication will then effectively set us up for the next aspect of the structure—the breaking of this pattern.

Until One Day...

"Until One Day..." breaks the pattern that we just set up.

- Once Upon a Time, a fish and his son lived on a coral reef in Australia

  - And Every Day, the father protected his son from the dangers of the open ocean

  - Until One Day, the child ignored his father's warnings

- Once Upon a Time, a farm girl lived on a rural Kansas farm

  - And Every Day, she dreamed of going away, anywhere, even over the rainbow

  - Until One Day, a tornado carried her and her dog far away, over the rainbow

"Until One Day" is the counter to our "Everyday" and, in a three-word phrase, defines why this is a story, rather than an anecdote or a series of random or coincidental events.

By establishing a pattern and a break in that pattern with "until one day," we set our audience up for the expectation that something different, perhaps even interesting, will happen.

A common issue with storytellers is not knowing where to enter their stories, and how to make them feel "like a story." This is an excellent place to begin. Find the inciting incident—the moment or decision that changed something and then ask yourself—what pattern might this have changed? We aren't all so self-aware as to realize the patterns and cycles that consume us. But observed through the lens of "Until One Day…" that happenstance may just take on a flavor of its own.

I recommend taking the same story idea and playing with different points of entry via this gauge.

Here are some variations of another story of mine:

- Once upon a time, I embarked on a five-week solo backpacking trek in Southeast Asia

  - (And every day) I am not the kind of person who enjoys sleeping naked

- – (Until one day) in light of the fact I would not be able to do my laundry easily for over a month, I decided to sleep in the nude…

- Once upon a time, I went to a wedding in Hawaii

  - – (And every day) I prefer the feeling of pajamas to being exposed/naked in bed (even when alone)

  - – (Until one day) I woke up in the hallway of the Waikiki Holiday Inn, completely naked…

- Once upon a time, I took a five-week sabbatical from my job

  - – (And every day) I looked for ways to "make it count" and have adventures

  - – (Until one day) I found myself naked at the reception desk of the Waikiki Holiday Inn…

These are all variations of the same story, the same memory, constructed in very different ways. Each can suggest a different way into the same sequence of events, yet each either tipping the information early, or allowing it to develop and arrive later in the narrative.

None are necessarily wrong. Each has its merits and, in the right situation, could actually lead to a good telling of the same basic story plot. This is just one example of how the start of the Story Spine can be explored and used to help ideate or develop the beats and bones of a story.

And Because of That…

At this point in the Story Spine, we enter the "second act," where, now that the pattern of "every day" has been broken, "one day," the character embarks on a series of cause-and-effect decisions, actions, or both.

"Until One Day…" like the rest of the Story Spine, does not need to be literally said, or paraphrased in the telling of the story, but the concept of "until one day" might be attempted to see how you can thread your characters' decisions and actions in a linear manner, each leading to the next.

- Until One Day, the fish's son was abducted by a human scuba diver

    – And because of that, he chased after the boat, venturing into unknown waters and parts of the sea he did not know

    – And because of that, he met a fish who offered to help him find his son

    – And because of that, she led him deeper into the ocean in search of the lost son

    – And because of that, they were followed by a band of hungry sharks…

While the Story Spine is typically drawn or written out with only three or so "Because of that" statements, it's an open-ended exercise— encouraging the storyteller to add as many complications and discoveries as needed to the telling of the story.

"Because of that" does not just have to be a physical action. An action or decision can be made and "because of that," a consequence suffered. "Because of that, my boss called me into her office."

"Because of that" can also vary between the outer and inner life.

- Because of that, I felt embarrassed.

- Because of that (feeling of embarrassment), I searched for something to cover myself with, grabbing the morning paper that had already been delivered.

- Because of that (newspaper), I felt a bit less embarrassed and headed to the elevator…

The key concept is causality. When each step and each decision leads naturally and consistently to the next, we are hooked on the journey. We track your actions and decisions, whether we'd have made the same ones or not. We like seeing how other people navigate difficult or dubious decisions. They force us to ask ourselves "what would I have done in that situation?"

Remember also the idea of the "circle of probability." By setting up a circle of probability with the introduction of the "once upon a time," for this story, I am in Hawaii. We make certain presumptions—there would be tourists there, hotels, warm weather, maybe a laid-back attitude… If a Columbian drug cartel were to suddenly appear at this point in the story (it doesn't), that may seem surprising to some, out of place to others, and totally plausible to still others. By doing so, you serve to expand the "circle of probability" to now include drugs, drug lords, crime, police, and other factors that, until now, would not otherwise have entered into the audience's mind.

Also worth suggesting here is the concept of coincidence. In the realm of human experience, coincidence happens, or may seem to happen, quite often. By coincidence at this point, my mother could have come down the hallway of the hotel (she doesn't, don't worry). While it's possible that she could, to some this may push the boundaries of what they expect possible in the circle of probabilities.

If there is a need in your story to include a late-occurring coincidence, a good strategy is to plant a "seed" earlier in the telling that might allow for the inclusion of that element within the circle of probability—so that the character or coincidences appearance feels somewhat foreshadowed or introduced. More on that later.

The body of the story, these "because of that's," are where, often, the bulk of the storytelling occurs. The character(s) are tested, inner decisions are made, and revelations occur about who and why and how you deal with the situation.

The action will continue to rise through these phrases until they can rise no more, and we must arrive at…

Until Finally…

"Until Finally…" is, as you would expect, the climax of the story. The rising action can rise no more. The confrontation you feared would happen will happen. The door is slammed. The gavel falls. The airplane takes off without her on it. The point of no return.

When crafting or ideating a true story, "until finally" may actually be the first thing you think of when deciding to develop this incident into a story. For my Hawaiian sleepwalking story, the climax occurs when I am standing, naked but for the front page of the *Honolulu Star-Advertiser*, requesting a new key to my hotel room, and the clerk requests "some identification."

There is no more need for story after that point, just resolution, reflection, and perhaps perspective.

"Until finally" cannot come out of pure thin air. It must live firmly within the circle of probability you have already drawn. A new character couldn't or shouldn't materialize that will resolve or make everything right in the universe. My hotel clerk, a real character, is not present in the early scenes, but because it's a chain hotel which employs such staff, the idea that he might appear would not make someone jump out of the story's reality in a negative way.

If Big Bird showed up with a solution, that would be a different matter altogether.

And Ever Since That Day...

So, what is "Ever Since That Day?" in your story?

Resolution? No—we resolve the conflict with the climax (Until Finally…).

Epilogue? Perhaps—this could seem like an afterthought in the story.

I like to look at "Ever Since That Day…" as the balance to "And Every day…" at the start of our story spine. If "Every day" our character wanted to run away from home, "Ever Since That Day" she realized there's no place like home.

If "Every day" our character wanted to join the Academy (for starship fliers), "Ever Since That Day," he became known as one of the most esteemed and heroic pilots in the galaxy.

When constructing a story, this section of the Story Spine is an excellent place to find the beginning and end of your arc. What was the change that happened after the climactic incident? From there, can you reverse engineer an "And Every day…" statement to balance it?

In my "punched in the face" story, the "Ever Since That Day…" can be the way I approach driving (more carefully?) since the incident—which I can flop to make the "And Every Day" be "(And Every day) I, like many drivers, don't like getting tailgated. I'm prone to getting agitated when someone rides the back of my car. Worse, when they start beeping at me."

"Ever Since That Day" can also be what's changed in your life since this incident. Can be a perspective on the world, an attitude shift, an appreciation for something you didn't notice before.

In my "Cousin Norman" story, the inciting incident, Norman's unexpected death, has nothing really to do with my life situation. His life, while important to mine, was not consequential to mine or my family's other than our love for each other.

But when his death results in an inheritance for me, it becomes personal. That love and appreciation might have an unexpected financial reward—this "ever since that day" appears both unexpected but also supported by the information and evidence offered through the telling of the story. This is a case where it is not an equal balance between "and every day" where, in the case of the Norman Story, the "every day" might be "and every day I appreciated the quirky mannerisms of my maternal first cousin." The resolution "and ever since that day, I realize how much he loved me, and my brothers and children, as well as we loved him," by naming us in his will and allowing my children the financial means by which they can afford college. But more importantly, I realize how much we loved each other, and how much he is and will be truly missed.

The Moral of the Story...

In the story spine, a moral is an optional component. In a storytelling exercise, it's a valid question to ask oneself or another storyteller after hearing or telling one's story: What is the moral of the story?

In asking it, we jump "up" a level, from the specific situational scenarios explored in the individual narrative, to a greater or higher-level teaching. "The moral of the story is…be nice to your quirky cousins"

"The moral of the story is…appreciate the family and friends you have around you"

"The moral of the story is…in order to protect your family, you might need to let them out of your protective grasp."

"The moral of the story is…everyone's dealing with their own issues and situations, and the best we can do is try to understand and empathize with others."

Entire books can be (and have been) written on the topic of story structure. This may not be the ideal forum to dive into an academic discussion of every variety of alternate story structure, aside from making clear that the "Story Spine" is not always the idea form to tell a narrative story.

That said, I feel strongly that it is beyond helpful to the point of imperative that one understand what the spine of their story is before breaking it out and telling the story in alternative ways.

So, if the story spine is the classic "linear" format, then what would we define as a "nonlinear" story?

Nonlinear Stories

A nonlinear story would be, literally, a story in which the action does not unfold in a strictly linear fashion. This can take a variety of formats.

For a true story, the challenge is to experiment with and discover which format works the best for the specific story. No one format will work for all stories—and by simply applying a structure to a story, you are not necessarily aiding (or harming) the storytelling. You are simply exploring alternate ways of communicating the experience— and by doing so, will find one that both bolsters the dramatic and essential narrative spine, while also serving to balance the feelings you are seeking to elicit in your audience—be that laughter, empathy, education, or something else.

Here are some of the more common nonlinear structures you will see in live-true storytelling shows like *The Moth* with examples and use-cases that may inspire or encourage you to try them with your own story:

Petal Structure

The Petal Structure

The petal structure is so named for the illustration that usually accompanies it, showing three or more "petals" around a central core. The core is a unifying theme or message. The petals are individual and often isolated stories, all of which support or build on the central message.

This is an interesting and effective structure for stories that might feel "too short" to tell as a standalone story, but when combined with other similar experiences or stories, can add up to a greater and more effective whole.

It's almost an episodic format—"this one time…" you may narrate about an incident or occurrence when you had an interaction with someone that led you somewhere (or nowhere). Rather than following a story-spine type of "because of that" learning, this may terminate with a kind of "moral" or insight, followed by "another time" that also could terminate in the same moral or maybe a matured learning. Put together, if the multiple "petals" can feel unified, the collection of stories will hold up.

A cautionary warning for this kind of storytelling structure: it's nice when listening to stories to get a sense of where they are going, while not tipping your hand to reveal the specific surprise or outcome. When a storyteller seems to conclude a story and then launches into a new story, it can create "listener anxiety" of feeling like "oh no, I thought the story ended, but now another one began." In the petal structure, with a general sense that these short examples will bolster a bigger change, perspective, or learning, the audience can relax into listening to them.

A cinematic example of this style of storytelling is the Steven Soderbergh film, *Traffic*, based on a British miniseries of the same name. Rather than following one storyline, writer Stephen Gaghan's screenplay for this film follows several different stories, each with the same message—"the war on drugs is a failure." Interestingly, each of the stories inside of this format must have its own structure, though they can differ as long as the unifying thought or message is consistent.

Bookending

Sometimes also called "In Media Res" structure, bookending is a very popular structure used for short form and long form storytelling. The "big idea" here is simply to avoid a long on-ramp to the meat of your story by starting right in the middle—such as right before the climactic action.

"I'm standing on the edge of the Golden Gate Bridge, looking down at what could be my last view of the Bay."

What? Why? How did you get here? What's going to happen?

Before going to the next moment (and based on the fact that you're here telling me this story, I have a pretty good instinct that this was not the end for you), the bookending structure would have you rewind in time—perhaps two weeks prior. Perhaps two hours prior. Whatever is needed now to back-fill this exciting or interesting point that you've left us wondering about.

"Two weeks earlier, I had been accepted to law school. My parents always told me I would be an incredible lawyer. My dad was a trial attorney and the arguments he and my mother had were legendary. One time, I intervened and got them to listen to one another…"

We've gotten far away from the "climactic" scene with personal backstory here. The idea is to tease an idea, then step away from it to build understanding, insight, and drama, so that later in the telling, when we get to the moment on the bridge, we have that rush of insight and memory of all the things that led up to this moment.

And then we can conclude the telling with "I knew in that moment, that this was the wrong path for me. My heart wanted to study architecture and seeing the city from this point of view brought tears to my eyes. I enrolled the next fall in the Master of Architecture

Program at UC Berkeley. Today I run my own small firm. My father is on my board of advisors…"

I used this structure in my "Norman" story with a thematic cliffhanger—"I'm cleaning out my older cousin's apartment after he died and that's where I discovered that Norman had a secret. Let me tell you a little bit about Norman. Norman grew up in New York and had a thick New York accent…"

I tease the "Secret" but do not tell it until just before the end of the story. Why? I want the audience through the telling to wonder what the secret is! To play the game of trying to figure it out, like a whodunnit novel. In the end, I tell it, and it's a surprise to me (the character in the story) as well, I hope, as it is to the listeners who got a different surprise than they expected.

The other benefit of trying this structure is that it's a great strategy to try when your story is running long. Cutting out a lot of unnecessary lead-in and background info that we THINK is crucial to understanding the story gets us quicker into the details of the specific story.

It's hard to believe until you try, but we generally "get it" when we're dropped into a story—and with some careful backfilling at the moments when we need that information, we can be caught up with the who's and why's to understand all the background information.

Flashback

Another form of bookending is the more traditional flashback model. Rather than telling the story in a linear fashion, drop the audience into your world as it is, in the "now" of the story, backing up when the need for backstory information arises.

There is a beautiful cinematic example of this in Pixar's *Toy Story 2*. While Woody is the protagonist of the story, his fellow collectible toys, Jessie and Stinky Pete are introduced without much, if any, backstory at all. They are collectible toys, awaiting their moment of glory as a set of toys on display in a museum in Tokyo. Jessie is a "rootin' tootin' cowgirl" with a zest for life, but a paralyzing fear of going "back in the box." We don't know much about her until a critical scene in the film when Woody is considering abandoning the group to return to his own life and family.

At this point in the film, through a musical montage set to Sarah McLachlan's "When She Loved Me," we learn that Jessie too was a child's beloved toy who, over time, became neglected, forgotten, and ultimately abandoned. When we return to the "now," we have this heartbreakingly clear understanding of how she's lost everything once and how, in this moment, she feels she is being abandoned once more.

If we'd known this information at the outset of the movie, we would have a much different picture of Jessie—she would be dimensional and empathetic and, possibly, less believably "rootin' tootin' " in those fun introductory moments.

But saving that heartbreaking backstory for the right moment of the story drives Woody's decision-making process to stay in a way that we can all clearly understand and empathize.

In contrast, another Pixar film, *Up*, places the backstory of the central plot right at the start of the film. A ten-minute wordless montage tells us everything we need to know about cantankerous protagonist Carl Fredricksen through his youthful optimism, love, and the loss that situated him where we find him at the start of the story.

So, think of how you might tell the "now" of your story as the central "spine," inserting nonlinear background information or scenes as needed to flesh out the forces and factors that shaped the way you are making your decisions.

These flashbacks, like most storytelling devices, work best when told as specific and concrete examples that illustrate an emotion or character-defining aspect. Less effective would be a "flashback" of this kind:

"There were lots of times where my mom said things that confused me."

Nonspecific memories or flashbacks add little to your story—they do not support the narrative or any resonance for the characters. Better would be a moment in particular that illustrates, efficiently, the point you are making.

"When I was twelve years old, my mom dropped me off at summer camp. As I was kissing her goodbye at the window of her station wagon, she reached in her purse and handed me three lambskin condoms. 'I'm too young to be a grandmother.' Then she drove away."

Hero's Journey

In his seminal work *The Hero with a Thousand Faces*, Joseph Campbell introduced the world to the monomyth—a consolidated mythical structure that has, almost magically, imbued stories across time, culture, religion, and geography. Termed the "Hero's Journey," this circular structural system forms its own "Story Spine" of sorts, one that ends where it begins, but the character is changed on the inside forevermore.

In a Hero's Journey, the character goes from the "Known World" to an "Unknown World" where they struggle against obstacles, challenges, and even suffer defeat and death (literal or metaphorical) before returning home to their "new normal."

You will notice many parallels to the story spine in a Hero's Journey structure.

A nice aspect that can add depth and richness to your story is to ask yourself some "Hero's Journey" questions:

- What is the External Journey my character (or self) is on in this story?

    - The External Journey would be your outward goals—a job, a relationship, a prize, a task to be accomplished of any kind.

- What is the Internal Journey my character (or self) goes on?

    - The Internal Journey would be your inward state—What do you really want/need?

    - Very often, the inner need will prove to be the opposite of what the external journey was to discover. The external prize may be attained, but that is the beginning of the discovery of the character's personal transformation.

        › Think of Luke Skywalker in the cave facing Darth Vader. But when the mask comes off, it's himself inside that costume.

        › Think in opposing pairs—the external mission might be to make money, but the inner mission and change becomes the opposite—to help others in need.

This is a brief summary of the beats of a Hero's Journey tale:

Hero in "Ordinary World" (And Every day...)

Call to Adventure (Until One Day...)

Refusal of the Call (Hero chooses safety over adventure)

Crossing the First Threshold (Cannot turn back—must engage)

Challenges and Trials (Because of That... Because of That...)

The Innermost Cave and the Final Ordeal (Until Finally...)

Resurrection and Return to the Ordinary World (Ever Since That Day...)

The takeaway here might be that there is not a single "Structure" that fits all stories. Learning more about these and other story structures gives you additional options for how you might try to tell your story in a linear, nonlinear, or cyclical manner.

By putting your story, structurally, into one or more of these well-known story styles, you may find that your original version worked best after all. You may see your story from another point of view or notice an insight that you had overlooked before.

Looking at stories from alternate points of view can never hurt the process.

How to Decide Which Story Structure to Use?

With so many possible structures to choose from, how do you know which is the "right" one for your story?

1. Figure out the story spine—the linear version of your story.

2. Does the beginning "grab" the listener? Is there a hook that gets their interest right away? If not, try In Media Res, starting with a scene that will make them curious.

3. If the Beginning is fine, where does the story lose interest? Would a flashback or edit sustain the momentum or desired pace of the story?

4. Tell the story (to someone) using the new story structures until it starts to click.

5. Try several structures until the story achieves the desired impact.

Exercise: The Kenn Adams' Story Spine

Take a story idea of yours OR make up a story using the Kenn Adams' Story Spine:

Once Upon a Time _____

_____

_____

_____

_____

And Every Day _____

_____

_____

_____

_____

Until One Day _____

_____

_____

_____

_____

And Because of That _____

_____

_____

_____

And Because of That _____ .

_____

_____

_____

_____

Until Finally _____

_____

_____

_____

_____

And Ever Since That Day _____

_____

_____

_____

(Optional) The Moral of the Story is _____

_____

_____

_____

_____

Chapter 3

The Improvisor's Mindset

Improv Jargon

"The Get"

A suggestion from the audience to begin a scene. As in, "Can I get a location where two people might meet?"

Improvisation is a form of live theater in which the story, characters, and dialogue of a scene or game are created in the moment. Often improvisers begin with a suggestion or a "get" from the audience or some other source of inspiration to begin.

While this is not a book about improvisation, there are several key benefits to adopting what you'd call an "Improvisor's Mindset" for storytelling. On the surface, the craft of "true storytelling" might seem the inverse of improv—which has in its nature a somewhat freestyle spirit, where stories are invented on the fly rather than related from life experience.

In this chapter, we will briefly explore how the fundamental principles of improvisation, along with a few of its games and exercises, can be applied toward the craft of true storytelling.

These concepts are part of a growing movement known as "Applied Improvisation," through which the same kinds of games and group lessons used in acting and comedy training schools are being applied for diverse purposes such as group team building, art therapy, and disaster readiness.

It's common in talking or writing about the subject that the word "improvisation" alone can make people feel uncomfortable—that they will feel embarrassed or forced to be "on the spot." If this is you, you're not alone, but rest assured, these are concepts only, and the exercises are intended to build on the concepts, each of which is intended to free your best ideas from that little critic that lives in all of us. You know the voice, the one that says to do things later or that you're not good enough.

In an upcoming chapter, I will also explain how you can use the fundamentals of improvisation for group work, to give and receive feedback and constructive criticism in a way that can help push your creative ideas forward in a positive and uplifting way.

Saying "Yes, And"

If it's one thing most people are familiar with from the improv training repertoire, it's the fundamental concept of "yes, and."

When I participate in a feedback session—public review and discussion about a work in progress story—the concept of "Yes, and" extends beyond the creative to the respectful. Bob Kulhan, in his article, "Why 'Yes, and' Might Be the Most Important Concept in Business," explains it like this:

> *"'Yes, and...' encourages the articulation of the individual perspectives of each teammate, acknowledging the importance of each opinion, accepting the ideas for exactly what they are worth, and providing a means of collecting ideas without judgment."*
>
> —BOB KULHAN

Pablo Picasso is quoted as saying, "I begin with an idea. And then, it becomes something else." This defines improv for me. A mindset where you start somewhere—anywhere—and then you start looking at it, advancing it, and adding to it, and it becomes—something else entirely. Something you could not have imagined from the outset.

What happens when we say "no?" No is very important. It protects us. It keeps us safe. It prevents trouble. Saying "no" to the act of storytelling itself is a good thing, right? It prevents embarrassment, the ire of our friends and family that we may tell stories about, and the danger that we may upset or irritate someone else with our opinions or perspectives.

But what happens when we say "yes?" Yes is the path to adventure. To risk. To possibility. To discovery. To the unexpected.

Saying "Yes, and" takes practice. It takes training to turn off the little voice in your head that says, "that's a bad idea," and to convert it to just acknowledging, "that's an idea." And behind it, there's another idea. And behind that, another one. And through an increasing volume of "at bats" comes an increasing number of "hits."

So, we say "yes, and" when we ideate. Here's how "yes, and" works when you generate the first telling of your story—you start talking. Out loud, to someone else.

Jargon

"Ideate"[2]
i·de·ate / īdē āt/ verb
1. Form an idea of; imagine or conceive.
2. Think.

When you tell a story, any story, you are generally playing a "Yes, and" game. You say something, and then you say what comes next. You build on that, over and over again, until the story concludes.

If you're paying attention to the person you're talking to, even if they say nothing, that person is helping you. How? Through their body and face. When I tell my friend a story and she nods, smiles, laughs, or otherwise reacts, I am getting real time "feedback." When she looks at her watch, or her eyes drift away, or she asks a question that I already said earlier, I'm getting another kind of feedback—cues that there are problems with the story, or the storytelling. Or cues that she's having a rough day that has nothing to do with the story or me. She might be thinking about the lunch she forgot to pack for her kid or the vet bill that seems way too high. Regardless, my story failed to transcend the vet bills and forgotten lunches—meaning I am still getting important feedback!

•••

Here's a basic "Yes, and..." game you can play to practice the concept.

---

2 (Source: Oxford)

Rumors

Rumors is a basic "yes, and" game played by two or more people (though it can also be played alone!). The concept is to affirm the previous statement and heighten it by adding to the last idea.

In the game play, the focus is passed between partners asking if they've heard about a specific "rumor." Once the rumor has been heightened, both partners put their hand on their mouth and "giggle" over the rumor.

Then, the player who ended the last rumor begins the next one (to the next person in the circle, or, if played in twos, back to their original partner).

Example:

A: Hey Brad, did you hear about the barber, Mr. Jones?

B: Yes! When people come in his shop, his breath makes their eyes water! <giggle!> Hey Dave, did you hear the rumor about the kids across the street?

A: Yes! They were grounded for putting glue on everyone's doorknobs! <giggle!> Hey Brad…

B: …

Continue as long as desired.

•••

Here's the classic "Yes, and…" game. Like "Rumors," this game can be played as an individual, in a pair, or in a circle with more than two people. The idea in any case is to pass the "ball" around, building on the last idea, starting each successive phrase with "Yes, and…"

Yes, And (Game)

In the example below, I will again use two people (player A and B) to illustrate the flow back and forth. A trick to try is to go as quickly as possible, not pausing to think of something "good," but rather playing with the first idea in your head. To write this, I am going to type as fast as possible, regardless of the outcome:

A: This is a story about my birthday party.

B: Yes, and it had a space theme.

A: Yes, and everyone was wearing space suits, helmets, and alien costumes.

B: Yes, and when I walked in, I didn't know who anyone was.

A: Yes, and instead of yelling "surprise," everyone spoke in alien languages.

B: Yes, and the cake was bright green.

A: Yes, and Darth Vader, hiding inside the cake, jumped out and surprised me…

Build on the previous idea and discover where the story goes!

Word-at-a-Time Story

Here's a story-related way you can integrate the concept of "Yes, and…" into creating or developing a story. The concept of listening, accepting, and building on can work to make up a story, or to develop a real event into a more fully formed one. This game requires more than one person. Otherwise, you're just…writing a story.

Players stand in a circle, or in pairs/threes. Tell a story one word at a time. Each player provides only one word of a sentence. A player saying "period," although that is not necessary, can indicate end of a sentence.

This can be more difficult than it sounds, especially for novice players. Remember that everyone at some point may have to say "the," "and," "or," or the other "boring" words in order to move the story forward. People can have an idea in their head that the story will go in some direction and want to cram two words together "the ELEVATOR" instead of just "the." Trust your partner. Give and take. The story will (by definition) surprise you because you only have partial control of it.

A: Once	A: Be	A: Another
B: A	B: My	B: Boy
A: Girl	A: Prom	A: I
B: At	B: Date	B: Was
A: School	A: When	A: Sad
B: Told	B: I	B: Until
A: Me	A: Went	A: Her
B: If	B: To	B: Mom
A: I	A: Pick	A: Came
B: Did	B: Up	B: With
A: Her	A: She	A: Me
B: Homework	B: Had	B: To
A: She	A: Left	A: The
B: Would	B: With	B: Dance

An alternate or more advanced way to play is to gradually increase the number of words said by each participant in this pattern: 1, 2, 3, 4, 5, 4, 3, 2, 1. This way each person gradually says more and more, and then fewer and fewer words, until the story is over:

(1 word) A: Once

(1 word) B: Upon

(2 words) A: A time

(2 words) B: there was

(3 words) A: a green ogre

(3 words) B: who lived under

(4 words) A: the bridge behind my

(4 words) B: house. He longed for

(5 words) A: candy, so I scattered my

(5 words) B: Halloween loot over the edge

(4 words) A: of the bridge. He

(4 words) B: was so happy, he

(3 words) A: threw back a

(3 words) B: handful of gold.

(2 words) A: I said

(2 words) B: Thanks Ogre!

(1 word) A: The

(1 word) B: end.

This is also a fun way to practice the rhythm of storytelling. Since the whole story should conclude by the end of the pattern, you get a sense at the midpoint (five words) that the story should start moving toward a conclusion.

When you feel the shift into the "improvisor's mindset," you also feel the pull from a place of judgment and critique to a place of creative openness and opportunity. Train your brain to play and you open up a new realm of possibilities for the stories you can develop.

Exercise: "Yes, And"

Play as quickly as possible, not pausing to think of something "good," but with the first idea in your head. Write or type as fast as possible, regardless of the outcome, with a friend or alone:

This is a story about _____

_____

_____

Yes, and _____

_____

_____

Yes, and _____

_____

_____

Yes, and _____

_____

_____

Yes, and _____

_____

_____

Yes, and _____

_____

_____

Yes, and _____

_____

_____

Yes, and _____

_____

_____

Yes, and _____

_____

_____

Yes, and _____

_____

_____

Yes, and _____

_____

_____

Yes, and _____

_____

_____

Yes, and _____

_____

_____

Chapter 4

The Idea Mill

If it's one thing storytelling has taught me in my years of practicing and teaching it, it's that you've got plenty of memories and experiences that will make incredible stories—you just need to release them.

One of my favorite parts of developing a story is ideating all the possible stories I could mine for a particular topic. One of the keys to finding ideas is broadening our view of what might make a good platform on which to build a story.

If someone asks you to tell them a joke, you may draw a blank. Then, they tell you a joke and you go, "Oh! I know that one!" Stories can be the same. "I don't have any good stories." Then you tell them a story and they say, "Something like that happened to me..." and launch into a great story of their own.

Combining some earlier discussed philosophies, including saying "yes, and" to yourself and silencing the critic telling you, "that's a silly idea," let's revisit the game introduced earlier to unleash these ideas, *That Reminds Me of the Time*:

That Reminds Me of the Time

With a partner, the leader gives a single-word prompt to the group. Player A or B (whoever has a "hit" first) offers up a very short fragment of a memory of what that reminds them of:

A: (for the prompt "school") Ok. School. That reminds me of being scared my first day of kindergarten.

Player B listens to this and volleys back and forth, as quickly as possible.

B: My ex-girlfriend was a kindergarten teacher. That reminds me of the time I went to visit her class. It smelled like pee.

A: That reminds me of a time I was invited to give a lecture to a school, and I had no control of the kids.

B: That reminds me of skipping out of school and getting busted.

A: That reminds me of getting detention for forging my principal's signature.

A few notes for this exercise:

It's important that the players don't go into the entire story/memory. This is not for storytelling, but for ideation—shaking loose these fragments of memory by hearing something else that gets your mind working in areas it hasn't thought about for a while.

It's also important to know that while you are shaking loose a memory, you each have a job to do: setting up the next person with some kind of "yes, and" addition to their memory. It's not as helpful to say, "that reminds me the same thing happened to me!" That's saying "yes," but without the "and" component, you're not seeding the next memory.

Example:

A: That reminds me of getting detention for forging the principal's signature.

B: That reminds me—the same thing happened, but forging my parent's signature.

A: That reminds me of trying to copy my dad's crazy scribble signature.

B: That reminds me of the first time I tried to make my own "signature" instead of just writing my name.

A: That reminds me for some reason of copying band logos like The Doors and The Monkees on my high school notebooks.

My experience with this game is that, within just a few minutes, students generate a lot of possible story material while getting to know each other and things they have in common. One student recently told me he was going to try this the next time he had a date!

If there is time, I suggest following this exercise by encouraging the students to briefly write down ideas that came up during the game in case they want, later, to develop any of those memories into ideas.

"That reminds me of the time" is one way we can say "yes, and" when we ideate. In future chapters we will learn other games and exercises that help you "free your best ideas" from imprisonment in your long-term memory.

Exercise: That Reminds Me of the Time

With a partner or alone, take a single-word prompt and write (or say aloud) a short fragment of a memory of what that reminds you of.

Prompt: _____

That Reminds Me of _____

_____

_____

That Reminds Me of _____

_____

_____

That Reminds Me of _____

_____

_____

That Reminds Me of _____

_____

_____

That Reminds Me of _____

_____

_____

That Reminds Me of _____

_____

_____

Another useful technique is to "research" by asking friends who may have been with you at times that you recall as being "story worthy." They can help to shake off the cobwebs and remind you of stories from their perspectives.

Exploding the Prompt

What do you think of when you hear a storytelling prompt like "out on a limb?" Do you think of a specific time in your life that you did something dangerous or crazy? Do you think of a literal connection—like falling out of a treehouse?

"Exploding the prompt" means getting past the first, second, and third ideas that pop into your head. Dive deeper and plumb memories you may not have considered in a while. The concept I subscribe to is to go ahead and start with the obvious or boring or even the "bad" ideas. Getting the clichés and ideas that might lead nowhere out of your head and onto paper (or out loud), get them "out of the way" so that other, wilder, weirder, or deeper ideas may emerge. Ideating from the obvious to the not-as-obvious can bubble up ideas or memories that you would not have even considered if you hadn't gone looking for them.

When I try to think of a story to tell at a storytelling showcase, I like to start from a prompt—a word or phrase that would inspire and focus my mind. For many shows like *The Moth*, the show producers will publish the show's themes weeks or months beforehand, so you can look online to see what the topics are. I'll take the word and play this game with it: "*Explode the prompt.*" Here is a list of recent *Moth* themes: endings, ego, awards, & tests. Choose a word (I will use "endings" for my example). Break the word out into all the possible branching definitions or avenues that it might offer as possible definitions or correlations:

- Death of a pet

- Death of a loved one

- End of a relationship/marriage

- End of a job

- End of a lease or mortgage

- Ends of your hair

- End of the line

- Reaching the end of a course, class, training, or process

- Completing a creative project such as a painting, a poem, or a novel

- The end of a phase of life: pregnancy, childhood, college, graduate school

For each (or as many as possible) of the above, does anything come to mind that could be mined for story potential? Here are the ones that trigger memories or possible stories for me:

Death of a pet:
Teaching my kids about death with the death of their pet goldfish

Death of a loved one:
Discovering, after his death, that my cousin had a secret

End of a relationship/marriage:
Breaking up with the girl my parents wanted me to marry

End of a job:
Being fired from the post office for failing their driving test

End of a lease or mortgage:
Getting evicted while my wife was pregnant

Ends of your hair:
My five-year-old brother cutting his hair to resemble a beloved (bald) cousin

End of the line:
Falling asleep on the school bus

Reaching the end of a course, class, training, or process:
Driving school

Completing a creative project, such as a painting, a poem, or a novel:
Creating a cabaret show and taking it on tour

The end of a phase of life:
Pregnancy, childhood, college, graduate school
Kids losing their teeth, and their innocence, at summer camp

Select one or more that have potential to develop into a story.

By simply saying "yes" to the theme and building a list of potential stories, I've now given myself, in less than five minutes, ten possible stories I could develop to tell in a show. Are all of them necessarily worthy (or ready) for performance? Of course not.

The alternate approach I see often is that someone takes the theme and goes with the first idea that pops into their head only. They tell the story out loud, which doesn't go very well. They say "no" to the idea, and maybe to the idea of telling a story at all. "I don't have any good 'endings' stories."

Exercise: Play "Explode the Prompt"

Take a prompt and list as many possible branching definitions or avenues that it might offer. Then, for each branch, write a possible memory or association from your life that could be developed into a story.

Prompt

_____

Branch 1	Branch 2	Branch 3	Branch 4	Branch 5

_____

_____

_____

Story Ideas	Story Ideas	Story Ideas	Story Ideas	Story Ideas

_____

_____

_____

_____

_____

_____

_____

The Vomit Draft

*"If you wait for inspiration before you write,
you're not a writer, you're a waiter."*

—DAN POYNTER

*"Amateurs sit and wait for inspiration, the
rest of us just get up and go to work."*

—STEPHEN KING

Stephen King is a prolific storyteller and writer because of one simple habit—he writes every single day. It's tempting to put off doing anything we think will be a pain, even if it's something we "know" we should do—eat better, exercise more often, and write every day.

There's any number of life-hacks that can help inspire an otherwise uninspired writer or storyteller including:

- Two- to three-day writing retreats

- Thirty day write-everyday challenges

- Setting aside a "writing time" per day

One great advantage that I feel "storytelling" has over what we'd call "writing" is that no computer, pen, or paper is required. All you have to do is talk.

I always consider my first draft (or two, or three) of anything my "vomit" draft. Quick and dirty, cranked out as quickly and hastily as possible. Get it out of your brain via your mouth (or your fingers, if you're writing it down) without the critic on your shoulder caring if it stinks or not.

It's designed to stink! Vomit drafts are the impulsive version to cut loose from your conscious mind—to get it out!

I suppose it's easy to liken the vomit draft to the craft of improvisation itself—you don't want to stop to "think"—you just do. Be in the moment and get the ideas out so that you can discover what comes next. By disciplining yourself to allow this version to feel "disposable" you remove all that might seem precious about it.

Preciousness is the real predicament, I think. We know we have a good story. But waiting for the right time, the right words, and the right place to tell it are all just great excuses to not do it at all.

So, my suggestion is to *not* write it at first—just tell it. To someone (anyone). I take Lyft from time to time to get around town. Lyft drivers are generally friendly folks. And nearly always complete strangers. (One time my family had a Lyft driver that we discovered we *had* met before—when she was working as a *Disney Princess* on a cruise—and we had a picture of her on our phones!) I'll ask, "mind if I tell you a story?" Or if I want to be more transparent, I'll say, "I'm working on a story. Mind if I tell it to you for practice?"

It sure beats small-talking about "this weather we're having" or the score in last night's game! One great effect of telling your story in this way to a friend, a sibling, a complete stranger, is that they will generally do one of a few things in response:

- Give you feedback about what they liked about it.

- Empathize with you by sharing something it made them think about (and maybe tell you their story).

- Sit in shocked silence, so moved by the experience that no words can suffice to communicate how you have affected them.

Well, one can hope, right?

Building on the same concept, I generally suggest that my students
not write their stories down when they are working on them aside,
possibly, from some notes or the "beats" of the story. The "beats"
of the story are usually a succinct, one- or two-word tag for what
happens, scene by scene, in your story.

Why? The more we tell our stories out loud, the more we hear the way
the words come together, and the more we see the impact that have
on the people who hear them. When we say something and it makes
someone laugh, gasp, nod their head, or widen their eyes, we're doing
something right. When we say something that makes them squint or
tilt their head with confusion, or check their watch/lose focus, there's
some room for improvement. What's more, the trouble with writing
a first draft rather than speaking it, is that many have a tendency
to fall in love with their words. Once they're on paper, they take on
a preciousness that feels like something that's been accomplished.
We can be less likely to want to edit or revise something that we've
already written down…so try not writing it down at first—speak it
down! And after you've told it a few times, to a few different people,
try recording the beats and some key lines, and then tell it again.

Vomit drafts are a gift to your craft as a storyteller. They are
permission to fail, a license to not-commit, and a testing ground for a
story as you work it out, in real time, in front of friends and strangers.

Chapter 5

Giving and Receiving Feedback

Building on the concepts introduced in Chapter 3 (The Improvisor's Mindset), this chapter illustrates how you can use the fundamentals of improvisation for group work—to give and receive feedback and constructive criticism in a way that can help push your creative ideas forward in a positive and uplifting way.

This is a fundamental improv training game put into action for positive, and rapidly productive, feedback to creative storytellers, done and delivered in a way that is constructive and creatively inspiring.

Writers' Room

In the creation of TV and animated movies, it's common for teams of writers and producers work together, creatively collaborating on ideas to develop into stories.

By applying the "Yes, and…" principles, the focus for feedback to an idea shines a light on the brightest spots—what's working in the story, or in the storytelling—and encourages those aspects to develop and grow. Every story has parts that "don't work." Why spend energy "fixing" the problems when the same time can be efficiently spent finding the parts that DO work and building on those "successes?"

For this to work, the entire group needs to agree on what is meant or intended when we say the words "Yes" and "And." So, let's break the phrase into its components and define them.

When someone tells a story and we say, "yes" to it, what are we really saying?

Yes

- Affirmation
- Enjoyment
- Support
- You have our attention
- Understanding
- Belief/Credibility
- Comprehension
- Receptive to ideas

- Interest
- Curiosity
- Empathy
- ~~Agreement~~

~~Agreement~~

It is possible to say "yes" to a story or a storyteller WITHOUT agreeing with them. How? Stories are highly subjective—they represent our experiences, our beliefs, and our prejudices. They may touch a nerve and annoy or upset a listener. That said, for a productive group or individual note-giving session to adhere to our guiding principles, saying "yes" can still be honored—perhaps not by saying "yes" to the entire story—or to the parts you take issue with…but to the parts you did like! "I liked that it was a story about a mother and a daughter," is a way of saying "yes" to a story, about whose content you disliked, provided you did like the central relationship. If the content disturbed you, rather than saying "I didn't like the _____ scene," find a part that you did enjoy. "I believed the characters. They felt very authentic in the way you described them." Why? Think about this from the other perspective. To load a storyteller still developing her story with negative comments about what did NOT work is counterproductive.

Now let's looks at what are we saying when we say "And:"

And

- Plus
- Adding to the idea

- Enhancement

- Suggesting a new idea

- What if?

- Transition

- Connection

- Building on

- Exploring more about

In her book *Bossypants*, Tina Fey explains her take on the concept of "Yes, and":

> *"The first rule of improvisation is AGREE. Always agree and SAY YES. When you're improvising, this means you are required to agree with whatever your partner has created... The second rule of improvisation is not only to say yes, but YES, AND. You are supposed to agree and then add something of your own."*
>
> —TINA FEY, *BOSSYPANTS*

By framing a feedback discussion using "Yes, and," the feedback is forcibly framed toward what is working versus what is not. Consider the "working" parts the story's healthy seeds. Water those seeds, and watch the story grow around them. Stomp on the dying parts and you may well win the argument and kill those parts, but the entire story and motivation of the storyteller may wither as well.

If we focus our feedback toward the positive, and primarily on what IS working, by a seemingly invisible gravitational force, you will notice the storyteller and the story itself drawing itself toward what IS working—and doing more of that. Maybe that's more descriptive storytelling. Maybe it's more balanced narration showing both sides of a sensitive issue.

Example: While taking my storytelling class at The Writing Pad in San Francisco, Jeff Hanson told a story about a date he once went on. He was online dating and decided to meet the woman, a "former swimsuit model," for the first time in person. When he meets her, he describes her as "hot." "She looked just like her profile picture, which is pretty rare!" As the date unfolds, her flaws start to come out. She was in a pretty bad fire, where her hair caught on fire and burned 80 percent of her body. She had a complicated pregnancy and a scar that runs the length of her torso. She had two prosthetic legs. It's a dark dating story where Jeff gets grossed out and never sees the woman again.

In class, another student took great offense at the story. She felt it was mean-spirited and misogynistic toward the woman. She thinks Jeff is gross and a woman-hater. She is angry when she hears his story and wants to tell him so.

But, honoring the guidelines of the class, the offended student focuses her comments only on the parts of the story she can say "yes" to. "I liked the woman's character. I wanted to know more about her and the pain she must have felt with all of this tragedy in her life." "I also liked seeing your character squirm when you learned of her accidents. I think it's brave to show feelings that can be seen as shallow. I'm interested in hearing why you have these feelings about women."

Are these subtle (not so subtle) digs at the story? Perhaps! But they also focus the feedback on parts that she was both interested in AND curious about, as workable suggestions to the storyteller to give him notes on how he might improve and amend his story. This is far preferable to dressing someone down about what a bad person they are for having felt certain feelings, or for communicating them in a first draft of a story.

If we work to give our feedback with a "yes, and" point of view, we can actually help our fellow storytellers shape better stories, and draft improvements with every successive version. Insulting and criticizing the stories, and the storytellers, risks the opposite effect—creating shame for the storytellers and a feeling that they or their story is not worth telling. Any story, with the right direction, has the possibility of finding its way to be a personal, moving narrative that expresses an important experience for you.

That said, this can only go so far if helping a story without the storyteller being open to receiving this feedback! You can offer brilliant suggestions and "yes, and" 'til the cows come home, but if the storyteller doesn't want to hear you, your words will do no good.

Aikido

People generally receive criticism in three innate ways. It takes self-awareness, and choice, to change our patterns for receiving feedback. Provided the feedback is coming from the positively angled "Yes, and" approach, the receiving of the feedback can still feel like an attack or a criticism. For this reason, I suggest learning, teaching, and using a "receiving feedback" strategy based around the martial art of Aikido:

Don't Contend

One common way that people respond or reply to criticism, or an attack of any kind, is to fight back. When offering suggestions in a storytelling class, the dialogue may sound something like:

Teacher: "I liked the part where you came into the restaurant and I wanted to hear more about the setting—the atmosphere, the patrons, the food...what kind of restaurant it was. Things like that."

Student: "I've tried that, but it just makes the story too long. Plus, it wasn't a very interesting restaurant. Wouldn't add much to the story."

The student has fought back, explaining down the suggestion in a way that implies, "no." This strategy will, without a doubt, be successful (for them). If they keep up the fight against all the suggestions they receive, they will win the round and protect the story as it is. But they lose the fight. Because at the end of that feedback session, nobody will want to suggest any ideas—for fear or knowledge that they will be shot down. So, the storyteller goes back home to work on their story with no new ideas. They are left to bang their head on the wall and wonder why their story isn't getting any better.

Don't Defend

The other common way that people respond or reply to criticism is to do the equivalent of curling into a fetal position, blocking their ears, or building a wall around them. They tell their story and then, once the story has concluded, retreat into a defensive posture where, out of shame or fear of being hurt, they quarantine their attention and ignore the suggestions, ideas, and reactions we are having around them.

The room may be alive with great ideas zinging back and forth—Yes, and'ing the brightest spots and writing jokes, lines, and consolidating scenes to make the impact more powerful—all being missed by the storyteller, because she is hiding from it.

When the session concludes, she again will feel victorious. "I won! They didn't hurt me or force me to change my story!"

The next week, she returns to class and tells, effectively, the same story—with the same issues or problems as she had last week, looking for ideas of how to make it better.

The class looks around at each other. "Didn't we already do this? How come none of those great jokes or lines we suggested made it into the story? Were you even listening to our ideas?"

If you are going to block out the feedback you receive, you may feel like you've won in the moment—but the end result is that nobody will want to give you feedback anymore! We don't want our good ideas to be ignored. We want to feel listened to and appreciated as well. And if you *contend* or *defend* when receiving feedback, we will retreat as well, and the end will be a stalemate.

Blend

The best strategy and technique, then, for *receiving* feedback in one of these sessions is to use the Aikido technique: blend. As Earl Vickers describes in his essay, " 'Yes, and': Acceptance, Resistance, and Change in Improv, Aikido, and Psychotherapy,"

> *"Aikido's blending practice...resembles improv's yes, and practice...emphasizing being present in the moment, avoiding struggle, and viewing resistance as a gift; these and other parallels help provide an interdisciplinary validation of the underlying yes, and principle."*
>
> —EARL VICKERS, " 'YES, AND': ACCEPTANCE, RESISTANCE, AND CHANGE IN IMPROV, AIKIDO, AND PSYCHOTHERAPY"

Rather than contending or defending, the storyteller practices listening to it, writing it down, or even yes, and'ing it themselves.

Teacher: "I liked the part where you came into the restaurant and I wanted to hear more about the setting—the atmosphere, the patrons, the food...what kind of restaurant it was. Things like that."

Student: "Interesting idea. The restaurant was really odd. It was a themed place where they waitresses yell at you. Definitely a hostile environment for a first date. Thanks!"

Let the ideas and feedback flow around the room. The ideas may be good, or not. It doesn't actually matter. What matters is (to try) not to impede that flow-state of creative riffing with the story at the center. Your story!

If you don't want to "yes, and," at the very least, try to get out of the way of the ideas being suggested by recording them, writing them down, or acknowledging them in some other way (not ignoring or retreating/combating them).

At the very least, when the session is over, you will have a collection of ideas to consider when you are back to "work" on the story— somewhere to begin your next pass. The list of possible ideas to try can be just that—"what if" I tried describing that restaurant? Could add some nice comic color to the scene set up as I walk into the date.

I've found the single best part of this model, for both giving and receiving feedback, is that when it works (which it does, more often than not), the room truly lights up the way a good writers' room should. Creative and helpful ideas fly back and forth. People are sharing, laughing, and yes, and'ing left and right.

And the best-best part is that *all* of the ideas that are suggested, written, discussed, and described as feedback become—in the way I run a room—the intellectual property of the storyteller who inspired it. So, I will listen to your story, give you 100 percent of my best ideas that can make your story better, and when you use my ideas, the credit for the story goes to you. The story is still 100 percent your story, not "cowritten by my teacher and nine storytelling workshop classmates." It is still all YOU. You're the one who still has to do the hard part—integrating the ideas in a way that works and feels natural, authentic and true to you and the situation that you experienced.

And why? Why give our best ideas away without demanding credit? Because, when the time comes around later for us to tell our stories, this is exactly what we want in return. We want everyone else's genius ideas to help bring the genius out of our own stories. We readily exchange genius for genius. Inspiration to unblock us in exchange for our outside insights to your story's needs. Outsiders to a story don't have the benefit of having lived it—so we get to ask the questions that intrigue us: what was she like? Why did he act like that? What did her voice sound like? These questions, ideas, suggestions, and insights will activate our stories and strengthen them.

Because, like Aikido, we open ourselves to the reality of the suggestions (the class saying "yes, and"). As Vickers synthesizes:

> *"The Aikidoist blends with the attack energy and channels it in a new direction, often by executing a turn that leaves both people facing the same way. One is now looking at the situation from the attacker's point of view, without giving up one's own."*
>
> —EARL VICKERS, " 'YES, AND': ACCEPTANCE, RESISTANCE, AND CHANGE IN IMPROV, AIKIDO, AND PSYCHOTHERAPY"

Chapter 6

Color and Advance

With a solid understanding of the story spine, you can turn almost any event or incident into a narrative with a beginning, middle and end. Let's take an example of something that happened to me while writing this book: I accidentally turned off the lights in my house from another city.

(Once upon a time...) I was on a family vacation in Chicago.

(And Every day...) I had grown accustomed to lazily turning the lights on and off in my "smart" living room (at home) with a voice command "Alexa, living room off."

(Until One Day...) As a joke, I said "Alexa, living room off" in my hotel room.

(Because of that...) I remembered that I'd brought a portable "Alexa Dot" with us on the trip, which replied "ok."

(Because of that...) The lights in my house turned off.

(Because of that...) I remembered that there were houseguests staying over in our house who arrived the same day.

(Because of that…) I checked another "smart" device I had set up—a security camera in the living room, seeing that the guests were confused, in the dark.

(Because of that…) I didn't want them to know I was peeking in on them but wanted to help.

(Because of that…) So, I called, saying "I think I forgot to tell you how to turn the lights on and off."

(Until finally…) Using the camera app, I watched them successfully turn the lights on.

(And ever since that day…) I was very careful what I told my Alexa!

Not the most exciting or interesting story, I know. But a basic frame onto which I can start working. A great exercise I like to use to flesh out a story is one I learned as an improv game: Color and Advance.

Color and Advance

When played as a game, this works best with two players paired up.

Designate one person "Player A" and the other "Player B"

Have Player A act as the "storyteller" whose job is to invent a story from a suggestion.

Have Player B act as the "director," whose job is to interrupt the storyteller using, primarily, these two words: Color or Advance.

Color is shorthand for "add more detail"

Advance is shorthand for "move the action forward"

When coloring, Player A should describe a specific element of the story in as much detail as possible. Player B should identify the specific aspect to be colored by saying, "Color the _____" (e.g. "Color the mother character").

When the story is complete or time is up, have the participants switch roles.

The "Director" must never become a passive listener to the story. It is their responsibility to get what they want from the storyteller. When something interests them and they want more information about it, they say "color!" When the story is dragging, taking too long, or when they've heard enough description, they should interrupt the storyteller with "advance."

It's very important in this game to not be NICE. This isn't a game for actually hearing a good story (spoiler alert). It's to stress the balance between what happens and how it was.

I guide my students to use all their senses when coloring—Sight, Smell, Sound, Touch, Taste, and Emotion. "Color your emotions" should focus attention on how you felt at the moment. "Color the highway" might elicit "Cars whizzed by me, blowing giant gusts of wind in my face. A truck sounded like a jet engine when it passed.

This can work as a writing and a speaking exercise. I've had students tell me they "wish they could use this everyday" to get people to tell them more, or less, information. I tell them "you can!" Hear someone say something that intrigues you, why not try saying "color!" I'm sure they would be happy to tell you more.

So, let me give this a shot with an "Amazon Alexa" story—to build on the spine with some choice color.

(Once upon a time…) I was on a family vacation in Chicago. It was a two-week road trip, with my wife and two kids. We were going to five different cities, five different hotels.

(And Every day…) I had grown accustomed to lazily turning the lights on and off in my "smart" living room (at home) with the voice command "Alexa, living room off." It would wirelessly turn off two separate lights in the living room—both of which have hard to reach power switches.

(Until One Day…) Sitting up in bed one night, as a joke, I said "Alexa, living room off" in my hotel room. I was so tired from touring museums and the city all day, and called it, partly out of exhaustion, as if the computer might magically save me from having to get up and turn off the lights in the hotel.

(Because of that…) I remembered that I'd brought a portable "Alexa Dot" with us on the trip, which replied "ok." I'd brought along our portable Amazon Alexa for the trip because it could play music, tell you the weather, and act as an alarm clock.

(Because of that…) From her response, I realized that, though we were two thousand miles from home, the lights in my house turned off. This would, under normal conditions, have been uneventful. But just then…

(Because of that…) I remembered that there were houseguests staying over in our house who arrived the same day. It was Erin, my wife's college roommate, and Paul, her excitable eight-year-old son. We're a bit messy at home, so before we left, we set the house up for our guests—including a detailed five-page typed document explaining everything from the Wi-Fi password to how to lock the windows and doors and why not to leave anything in her car (as car windows are often broken to snatch anything that looks valuable).

(Because of that…) I checked another "smart" device I had set up—a security camera in the living room, seeing that the guests were confused, in the dark. It felt weird to check the camera—I did not want to spy on them—but remembered we had set the camera to look in on the living room since we'd be gone for so long.

(Because of that…) I didn't want them to know I was peeking in on them but wanted to help. Still, once you're watching an eight-year-old who doesn't know he's being watched, it's a bit of a comedy show. "What happened?! MOM! Did you turn the lights off??" I considered telling *our* Alexa to turn the lights back on, but my whole family yelled, "no!" We discussed what to do. If we just turn the lights on, they could get scared. And if we tell them we saw them or that we did it, we're super creepy people. My wife, as usual, had the right idea. "I will call to check in."

(Because of that…) She called, saying "I think I forgot to tell you how to turn the lights on and off." "Oh my gosh! We were just reading your document trying to figure out how to turn on the lights!" When we hung up, I asked my kids, "should we watch to see what happens?" All heads nodded in unison. We watched as the adorable, lisping eight-year-old stood next to our piano and said "Alek-tha, Living Room Light-th on!" like he was casting a spell in a Harry Potter book.

(Until finally…) As we watched them, using the camera app, successfully turn the lights on, they cheered at their success. We cheered with their success, and at our crafty way of both getting the into, and out of, trouble.

(And ever since that day…) I realized that night, I've filled my home and my life with devices and conveniences that are surveilling me twenty-four hours a day. I'm not a tin-foil hat wearing conspiracy theorist or anything, but for the rest of the vacation, you better believe I was very careful what I told my Alexa! I am also happy that I have these devices. There were strangers in my house and, inadvertently, thanks to those gadgets, I can know twenty-four hours a day what kinds of shenanigans are happening when I'm not home.

Again, maybe not the best version of that story, but it's a vomit draft. I story-spined it, and then I enhanced it (using color and advance, filling in details, emotions, and reflections).

In the end (of this draft, at least), it's starting to take shape! There's the start of a narrative (what happened), and a more realized world (through the details, dialogue, and emotional reflections of the narrator).

My next step here would without a doubt be to tell it out loud. Not reading it, but telling it as best I can remember. If I was to read the above as a story, I'd get locked into the words and descriptive phrases I'd chosen to type up. If I tell it from memory, those phrases would come out differently. Better? Who knows until I've said it?

The next draft would be some hybrid of those last two…some elements as I planned it, and some that will come out in the moment. The ideal version of this story will strike a balance between what happened (advance) and how it was (color). When we color and advance our storytelling, we give our audience more than the information; we share with them the experience.

Exercise: Play "Color and Advance"

Designate one person "Player A" and the other "Player B."

Player A invents a story from a suggestion.

Player B interrupts the storyteller using the words: "Color" or "Advance."

Interrupt often! After two to three minutes, switch roles.

ALTERNATE (Solo Version): Using a clock with a second hand or a stopwatch (or any way of tracking time), tell a story, out loud, and alternate color and advance every ten seconds—coloring the last thing described, or advancing from wherever you are in the description.

Chapter 7

Sticky Stories

Calibrating Our Stories

We've entered the crucial second phase of storytelling development—the editing and reworking phase. While many people dread this part of any endeavor, I love it. I think this is where you get to roll your sleeves up and move from the "ideation" brain into the "diagnostic" brain—looking at your story from different points of view and turning knobs and levers to tweak it.

There are a number of ways of doing this. As mentioned in previous chapters, one way is getting it on its feet by telling the story! Here are some ways and places I've tried this:

To Myself

Sometimes I just want to hear what the story sounds like coming out of my mouth. To do this, I spend a fair amount of time in my car, so I turn on the voice recorder on my phone and tell the story while I drive!

Very often, I don't listen to the entire recording, or even to any of it. So why record it? For me, it's psychological. If the phone isn't listening, then nobody is listening. Having something there that can "hear" me makes me feel like I need to keep going.

Almost always, something WILL pop out that surprises me— something I did not plan or expect.

When it is safe (i.e., when I am no longer driving!) I will go back and try to note where or what that unexpected part was to work it into my outline.

To a Friend

Another great way to test out your story is to tell it to a friend, a relative, or someone else whose opinion and taste you trust.

When they give you feedback, remember they are probably not trained in my style of "yes, and," so it's up to you to use your Aikido skills to take their comments, even if they're not constructive, and do your best to feel listened to and appreciated.

If they do have good notes, and time, I sometimes ask if I can tell them the story again (right away). This time, try to, on the fly, incorporate the "big notes" that stuck with you and—see what happens. They will start to see the "mechanics" of the storytelling in play (since the surprises of what happens are gone) and you might get a few additional thoughts from them after the second telling.

In Class

Small groups and classes like the ones I teach are great opportunities for storytellers to practice their craft and give each other feedback.

I suggest setting a time limit for each participant so that one storyteller doesn't use up the whole session.

Another way to optimize time in a group is the "speed dating" style—pair up and tell your story to one person at a time for feedback one-on-one.

Go to an Open Mic

With the popularity of storytelling still on the rise, there are numerous open mic style storytelling events in most cities every month. In larger cities, there may be several per week.

The format is often "hat draw" where you are not guaranteed a spot— you must put your name in and hope it gets pulled.

When working on a story, there are a few "systems" I enjoy using to strengthen my stories. These are not tools used to ideate a story as much as they are useful for, when you have a story in progress, measuring what's working best and reinforcing it.

SUCCESS in Storytelling

I am a big fan of the Heath Brothers (Dan and Chip Heath), a pair of authors and teachers who work at Stanford and Duke Universities. Their book *Made to Stick: Why Some Ideas Survive and Others Die* really "stuck" with me. It's one of the best books on effective communication I have ever read.

In it, they present case studies of stories, marketing campaigns, and brands that succeed because they are able to stand out by leaving a lasting "sticky" impression. Brands like Apple, McDonalds, Southwest Airlines… Brands in crowded fields can differentiate themselves with a strong point of view and a number of common unifying traits.

There are many concepts from their book primarily targeted toward marketing and advertising that overlap with storytelling. One is the goal to overcome the "curse of knowledge" where the storyteller or presenter has information in their head that they assume the listener can also infer. They might predict that their listener will "get it" more often than they can, based on the fact that it's a story they know, have experienced, and can remember.

By adapting Dan Heath and Chip Heath's "SUCCESS" system for storytelling, you can edit your stories to be more interesting, actionable, and memorable.

Here is a brief breakdown of the steps and how they can be applied to measure and assist in editing your story:

Simple

Does your story have a single, understandable, through line? Can you summarize your story in a line like, "my son's tooth falling out made me realize I was having trouble letting go of his childhood"? Or "getting punched by a mother at my kids' elementary school changed the way I drive"?

This does not need to mean that the story itself is "simple." The plot and detailing of the story may be quite complex, but in the end, we should gather that a single arc of change has occurred, and the character has been transformed or made to realize something has changed.

If there is not a simple core and there are multiple threads, this may be an opportunity to try removing the emphasis on the second or third threads—to make the primary focus the heart of the story.

Here is an example I see often. Many people feel like they have more than one great story to tell. So, they tell a story, but then before it can end, or maybe after it already technically did end, they will continue, "and then one day I decided to move to Africa..." Wait, what? The story ended, and we had a lovely satisfying ending. But when I hear "until one day" show up at the end of a story, my PERSONAL story spine tingles and I want to scream, "stop!"

So, look for the simple core of the story. Or reverse engineer it.

Say you want the story to be "about" something that it's (currently) not. By writing or crafting what the simple core is, make edits to the story. Try removing whatever is not supporting or necessary for that core message. Does it help or hurt?

Universality

Your stories are 100 percent yours. You come from your own life experience and nobody is quite like you. But regardless of that, even when you have experienced something truly unique, it's important for your audience to find some connection to it. This is what we mean by "universal." What is the universally understandable aspect of your story that we can connect with?

Here is an example from Jeff Hanson. Jeff has lived an extraordinary life. From a childhood in rural Wisconsin, he migrated to Minneapolis, married his sweetheart, and transplanted to the Bay Area. Life happened and children, divorce, and job changes started him on a path of transformation and self-discovery.

One of Jeff's stories mesmerized and baffled me. He enrolled in a rather intensive self-help seminar in a rural area. Part of the program involved sensory deprivation and mind probing with sensors under extreme conditions including "listening" to his own mind "waves."

The whole story seemed crazy to me because I could not put my finger on any universal aspect of it. It felt so far-fetched and vague that I assumed it was invented.

But upon further development, the story revealed something I could grasp onto. Jeff was confused, afraid, and searching for answers. This I could relate to. He was skeptical of the program, even if the methods were unorthodox. That too I could get behind. By acknowledging that we're entering an unusual world and seeing it through his eyes, I could relate to the experience of trying something new and hoping for the best, even when the tools and techniques seemed unusual.

Once Jeff's story started including the point of view of his reactions to the world, I felt more comfortable going down the rabbit hole with him to the strange places to which he was willing to try going. In fact, it became fun, from that point forward, to hear how strange it was, because I could relate to Jeff's interest in it. I too take interest in new things.

Check your own story for "universality." Is there something in it that anyone could relate to? An emotion? A relationship? This will keep your audience engaged while you relate your specific experiences.

Concrete

Concreteness in storytelling usually emerges through the specific details we choose to include. "I got on the bus" is not a concrete detail. It is generic, and in the mind of everyone who listens or reads, that bus will look, feel, and seem different, based on his or her life experience. "I climbed the three steps to the yellow school bus, passed the smiling driver, and noticed there was only one seat left, way in the back, where the bullies sit." Now we have a visual, and some concrete feelings that give us a sense of where you are and what it's like in this introduction to the new location.

When we play "color and advance" we are playing with concrete details. Using our senses and our emotions, we are taking the generic, "I walked into her living room," to the specific, "The living room had cathedral ceilings and an entire wall was made of glass, looking over the Marin country redwoods."

Credible

I've seen amazing stories told at *The Moth* get average to low scores because the judges did not believe they were true. These were carefully woven narratives with rising action, surprising twists, and satisfying conclusions. And they scored in the low eights (out of ten). Why? When we tell a true story, our audience expectation is that it will feel true.

So how do we gain credibility?

Tell the Truth

First, let's assume that what you are talking about *is* true—that it happened to you and that you can relate that memory with some degree of accuracy. If that is the case, you are on the right track to begin with. Making a fictional story feel credible is a different challenge. If you were at a party and telling this story to someone, you likely would tell certain parts with a kind of scripted "this is how I always tell this story" kind of manner. But other parts, other details, they may just arise in the moment as you remember them in the telling.

Seeing you remember the story, being amused by the story, or being affected by your own story, because it's true, and it's affecting, and it's amusing, will make your audience believe you. Resist the impulse to make your story "more interesting" and stay with what feels the truest.

Be Imperfect

It's hard to explain why a smoothly executed narrative presentation of a true story loses credibility. Perhaps it is because when the storyteller can execute an unblinkingly perfect recitation of what is clearly a rehearsed and polished monologue, the audience loses the sense that this is a true story—and rather evaluates the storyteller as an actor delivering a soliloquy.

It's a catch-22 situation. Many writers and storytellers value crafting their words and feelings into phrases that can land with impact and resonance—so why should they jettison their talents to deliver a less polished version of their story? Because the audience will believe it's true when it feels true.

This is not to say that having a crafted story is bad. I think the best stories are the ones that are developed, crafted, and tested before and during a performance. The tactic I suggest employing is to harness that preparation and to be open to the spontaneous. Allow the story to drift, to slip into the "remembered" territory, and allow yourself to be imperfect in the telling, while knowing your beats and landing those impactful phrases and lines that capture how it was with literary flair.

Details

Credibility also comes out of the ridiculously specific details that only you are capable of including in your story. In my story about "Cousin Norman," I describe that Norman was a good storyteller. That is a generic statement that gives us no real information about him— everyone tells stories. Then I follow it up with a side-story anecdote:

Norman was like six and a half feet. He had giant glasses and giant ears and a giant nose, and he would tell these stories, "Oh Corey, I gotta tell you about this wonderful movie that I saw. It was called *Seven*, but it was so dark. Corey, it was dark, dark, this is a dark movie. When the movie was over, I was looking for my sunglasses. I had my sunglasses *on*, Corey."

All of the above, in addition, is narrated in Norman's thick New York accent, being that character of Norman as I relate this memory. If the audience didn't believe this was a true story before, they're more likely now to get their own image and picture of who this man is as I tell more details about his life.

Find the details that can situate the listener into the world of your story. This might be color as you establish a new location (the smell of cat pee hit me like a wall), a choice physical description of the character (his long hair and swastika tattoo), or a story-within-a-story (like Norman's movie-going experience). Details add credibility, while also reinforcing the universality ("I know someone just like that!").

Performance

How you tell your story is another way to gain or lose credibility. One of the regulars at the Berkeley *Moth* shows is Eva Schlesinger. A frequent winner, Eva has a high-pitched monotone style that is as unnatural as one can imagine—yet the audience loves her. She breaks the "imperfect" rule in every way—every word of her story is carefully chosen, expertly timed, and delivered with deadpan seriousness.

Her stories are full of details that make them richly credible. And she never fails to land a solid punch line to wrap up her tales. Though Eva has an exaggerated delivery, her stories, such as one about trying to buy a can of water, usually enchant and win over the audience.

Eva is a bit of an exception to the rule. By crafting this deadpan character, she is able to let the material speak for itself and the audience falls under her spell. For others, when the story feels too much like a performance, they may feel disconnected from the teller and lose credibility for the story being told.

In the end, credibility is some combination of the above attributes. By choosing specific details to include in your true story and delivering them with either flawed imperfection or flawless precision, your audience will "buy" that this is a true story.

As you work to improve your own story, look for these traits: Does this feel true? How can I enhance the details in the telling, or in the performance, to help my audience believe that it happened, and that it happened to me?

Emotion

We are emotional beings, and universally susceptible to the same feelings. We love, fear, surprise, grieve, delight, and worry—and when we experience a story that conveys and elicits these emotions, we appreciate it all the more.

Storytelling, like theater, music, and art, works best when it makes us feel something. So how can we turn this dial in our own stories?

Describe the Emotion

In addition to telling us what happened, walk us through what it was like at the time.

"I was terrified. Standing naked, alone in the hallway, I had nowhere to hide and I wanted to cry so hard that I laughed at myself."

Nearly every encounter can be laced with an emotional beat. Give your listeners a sense of what it felt like for you, in those happy or dark moments. We will gain empathy for your character and come along on whatever ride you take us on if we can relate and empathize with you.

Revisiting my son Henry's version of the "punched in the face" story, I noticed much of his telling of the story stays in the third person—about what I did, or what the woman did. Then he puts himself into the story:

And then she got really mad, "don't tell me to take a deep breath." And I was scared because I didn't know what she was gonna do. So, then my dad's like, "I have children in the car."

Narrating your own emotional state puts us in your shoes. We will understand that state of mind and increase our level of involvement in the story.

Feel the Emotion

Another way to convey emotion, as storytelling is a performing art, is to feel the emotion. If you are enjoying a moment in your own story, and we can tell, we are likely to enjoy that moment as well.

If you have to slow down because this part is painful to remember and to retell, take your time. We are in no rush. And your feelings are important. They are credibility embodied in the teller, as your emotions telling the story connect us to the reality of reexperiencing this story through telling it to us.

The emotion "slider" in a story can be nuanced. We certainly don't want to feel manipulated by a story that the storyteller is "trying" to make us cry. But when there is sincerity to the feeling and the telling, we feel more connected to the story we have heard.

Stories

This may seem a redundant point to make, but it's important, whenever crafting or editing a story, to remember its essential function as a STORY.

Does it have a beginning, middle, and end?

Does it follow some kind of story spine structure?

We will feel more connected, and apt to remember your story when it is, at its core, a story.

Not a list of things that happened when you studied abroad.

Not a stand-up comedy routine.

Not a set of statistics that tell us how common this infection is for newborn babies.

Take the time to craft the rising action and conclusion of the story if it's not there, to improve the overall experience of listening to it. Your story must have a setting (Once Upon a Time…), a protagonist (you), a struggle (because of that…because of that…) and a sequence of connected events that leads to a discovery or change (ever since that day…).

At its very core, you have two fundamental challenges to hook your audience in your story—their curiosity about:

What's going to happen next &

How is it going to end?

If you can keep your audience engaged in these two questions, you have them hooked and can carry them through to the conclusion. What's more, they are more likely to remember and even retell your story later.

What's more, the more personal your story is, the more people will connect with it. If this is a story that makes you the infallible hero with nothing to lose or gain, the less we will care to hear about it. It fails to be a story at all—it's bragging about a conquest or an example of how clever and creative you are.

Surprise!

In Dan and Chip Heath's *Made to Stick*, they say that "unexpected" moments capture our attention and imagination because we do not see them coming. They use an example of a 2001 car commercial for the "New Enclave," a car with remote control sliding doors and a full view sunroof. As a happy family cruises down the street in their new minivan, another car barrels into it with glass and metal shattering all around. "Didn't see that coming? No one ever does."

It was not a car commercial after all. It was a safety commercial from the Department of Transportation.

When you start to tell a story to your audience, you establish some expectations based on the information you are telling and based, perhaps, on you: assumptions they might be making based on your age, race, gender, attire, or other factors.

This is an opportunity, in many cases. You can set up, or predict, what your audience would expect to hear about this particular topic or in this kind of story—and then surprise them with the unexpected or counterintuitive things that happen.

How can we do this with a true story? You know what happens—if that's the unexpected thing, then reverse engineer it—what would set them up to expect something different? Something that's not a car accident—like a happy family driving in a stereotypical minivan commercial!

Cousin Norman left me a large inheritance—a surprise to me and to everyone who knew him because of the frugal life he led. If the only clues I give in the story are about his frugality, this might over indicate that he's going to give the inheritance. So, the details are indicated to create the expectation that the secret has more to do with his personal life. He had a secret family! Or that his secret was creative. He had written a bestselling novel!

Moth Principles

The good people at the "Moffice" (the Moth Office) have been kind and forward thinking enough to include some helpful tips on *The Moth*'s own website for storytellers.

As I did with Dan Heath and Chip Heath's book, I will build on their suggestions with my own for how to apply them to reworking your own story.

As with the SUCCESS system, these are intended not so much as ideation exercises or inspirations, but rather a metric by which you can gauge or measure your own story to build up the weaker or thinner parts.

Simple and True

Can you summarize, in a word or two, what your story is about? Sometimes when I am teaching, I will hear a story and put it to the class in just this way: "What is that story really about?" The answers are often surprising to the storyteller. She may have just told a silly story about helping a friend in a wheelchair out of a muddy beach while her friends stood by laughing at her. And the class will say that was a story about "friendship," "loyalty," and "selflessness."

You may not actually know what your story is about until after it's been told. The events of your story are not what your story is "about." It's about something else.

The Moth shows have a theme—Age, Endings, Betrayal, etc. But go to a StorySLAM and listen to ten true stories about Age and you will see the topic or prompt for the show is not what the show is about. Other themes like Family or Overcoming Hardship will emerge through these completely disconnected stories.

Look at your own story, or tell it to someone and ask him or her "what was my story really about?" And then, armed with that insight, look back over your story. How or where might you add, omit, or improve the material to support, challenge, or build on that simple, true message?

Universality

Building on the earlier mention of the same bullet point, adding or enhancing universality to your stories may be in the subject matter itself.

Is your story about a specific incident, like a vacation you took with your family to the beach?

I have a story like that, where my father embarrasses me by snorkeling nude in the Caribbean. While this specific incident likely did not happen do you, I can probably guess that you've been embarrassed by a parent or relative in the past. So, the universal concept "my family embarrasses me" links the storyteller with the audience.

I have found this to be the case for even the most far-fetched premises or for stories about which I have no personal experience with the events in the story. I have never been to outer space, and I have no Jedi powers, but the struggles, wants, fears, and hopes of Luke Skywalker are universally relatable.

I am not a fish, and though the plot of Pixar's *Finding Nemo* is fantasy invented by humans, I can relate to Marlin's protective instinct toward his son, his dedication to finding him against the odds, and Nemo's journey from innocence to experience.

Find the aspects that anyone can relate to and build on those, even when the specific happening in your story is peculiar and specific. Storytelling doesn't have to be a "you had to be there" experience if you can connect the audience with the emotions and relative human feelings that you felt.

Vulnerability

We spend most of our lives being the hero of our stories. We represent ourselves as strong, capable, intelligent, sensible, talented, and whatever other attributes we want to be seen as. When we are on a job interview or a performance review, we typically represent ourselves as such—worthy of the job, or the promotion, or the recognition.

Here's a story I heard recently in a class, told by Anthony Muscarella:

"When I was in kindergarten, I liked to steal stuff. I was friends with Tina and Sandy, but Tina was a bitch, and this story isn't even about Tina. Sandy's dad used to import those laser pens with the really strong laser light that you use for presentations. So, when I was at her house, I stole one of those pens. And the next day, on the school bus, I took it out…"

The character in this story is not what you would call "heroic." He is actually kind of unlikable. He calls his "friend" Tina a "bitch." He admits to stealing. He sets up the story in a way that we are expecting something terrible to happen. And I was hooked.

By exposing his own vulnerabilities, admitting his faults, opinions, and criminal tendencies, I'm very interested in his story. What's going to happen? He's trouble, and he knows it. This story is going to be good!

Sometimes I hear stories where the storyteller presents themselves as "above" the events of the story. They present themselves as some kind of "outsider" where something happens "to" them and it was "amazing!"

This story often follows this pattern:

I always was fascinated by _____. So, one day, I took a trip to a faraway place and I encountered _____. And it was AMAZING!

This is not a story. The character in this story is not relatable, not knowable, not likable, because she is not vulnerable. She is above the subject matter. She is a student of the topic, interested in it, and remains as such throughout.

When your character is impervious to harm, to emotion, and to consequences, we will have little or no empathy for her. When someone stands up and tells us how great they are, how smart they are, and how interesting they are, my first thought is, "oh, really?" And I start to look for holes. Flaws. Gaps.

Because we are all vulnerable. We all worry, cry, and fail. And when we let the audience in on those traits, those feelings, and those experiences, we are not diminishing ourselves in their eyes—we are leveling the field. We are like them. Or we are beneath them, and by being so, we invoke empathy, sympathy, or understanding.

So, instead of trying to impress my audience with my life experiences, I like to lower my status. Everybody likes an underdog story. We are happy to see you succeed, to triumph, and to learn. And to get there, we need to reveal our vulnerability in the situation so that the audience can root for us to get there. If we profess confidence that we knew the answers all along, and we were right—well, that's not a journey, that's not a story, and that's not very interesting.

I'm not trying to say that I'm a misanthrope who does not want you or your experiences to be positive. Quite the opposite. I cheer for your successes, your learnings, and your overcoming obstacles. But show me your fears, the peril that you found yourself in, and the risk you took, so that I can celebrate the victory over it.

All this is to say, stories are about change and about being affected by circumstances. If you are unchanged or unaffected, the story is not a story. And the more you reveal your mistakes and weaknesses, the more we will care about you and root for you to overcome the odds.

Specificity

In the last section, we spoke about using "concrete" details in your stories. In this matrix, we term it, similarly, "specificity." What are key specific moments, details, or aspects that make this incident, event, or encounter uniquely identifiable?

Describe the room as you enter it (the color of the walls, the art that's decorating it, the smell…)

Speak in the character's voice (respectfully—voices/accents should generally not be punch lines because they have an accent from another culture or country)

Slow down the details of a climactic action (don't rush through it)

Give a concrete number of people in the situation (not "lots of people were standing around")

My student Milton Schuyler has a story about when he was a house painter in the 1970s. On a fateful job, done while battling a stomach flu, he forgot the paint bucket was still on the ladder of the just-finished room when he moved the ladder to leave the job, after having already pulled up the drop cloths from the floor:

"I very carefully come back down the ladder and run to the bathroom. I come back out (this was a longer bathroom trip) and I get the ladder and I move it. And the gallon of paint flies down on the glass. All over the woodwork on the glass, drips down the windows, bounces onto the dark, wide-plank wood floors, and bounces up over by the furniture. I get down on my hands and knees, crying…"

The specific detailing of the mess Milton had made creates heightened sympathy for him, as we see in our minds' eye the chaos this mistake has caused. This sets up the climax and resolution of the story—will he get it cleaned up? How? Will he get caught?

The more vivid the details you can add to your story, the better the audience can see the movie playing in their own heads to match the one you want them to see. Like a big blank canvas, the audience can only see what we tell them to see. They will see nothing, or they will imagine their own version of your world until you give us reason to see, think, or believe otherwise.

Set Up the Stakes

Milton's painting story begins with him telling us he is living job-to-job. Painting one house interior at a time and relying on word of mouth to get his next job, his next rent payment, and his next meal.

When he gets the job in this story, the homeowner is very demanding. She is going to be back in a week, on call at the hospital. "The job must be done by the time I get back." Milton comes down with a stomach virus the week of the job. But, to satisfy both his needs (food, shelter, money) and hers (the job must be done this week), he works through the illness, taking frequent bathroom breaks as the virus works its way through his system.

When the bucket comes crashing down to the floor, covering the entire room in green paint, we are as devastated as Milton is. We hurt for him. We feel his pain. And we worry—how will he ever get out of this mess?

All of this has built the suspense because this story has very high stakes. The "stakes" of your story are what you have to gain or lose. What happens if things do not go your way? What happens if things do?

The stakes in Milton's story are simple—if I mess this job up, I can lose my apartment and my reputation as a painter. I'll never work again.

The third act of this story—Milton avoids a live-in nanny (Don't go upstairs. Everything is still wet!) and races to a hardware store to buy paint thinner, cleaning rags, window cleaner, and furniture polish.

As he restores the entire room to its pristine condition, we learn a thing or two about painter "tricks of the trade." We admire his creative problem solving in the midst of a crisis. As we sigh with great satisfaction and relief when the homeowner returns and glows about what a perfect job he did. "I'm sending you a tip, and a referral to a friend of mine who needs her house painted next week."

He gets out of the jam he's put himself into and lives to see another day, another month's rent, and another client.

If we do not know what is important, we will not care about the outcome. Let's do a "bad" version of Milton's story:

"I used to paint houses. I was great! I had lots of clients, and a perfect reputation. One time, I dropped the can of paint on the ground. But it was no big deal. I cleaned up the mess because I know how to deal with these situations. The homeowner loved the job I did and even gave me a big tip."

Loses something, right? Similar sequence of events, but without the stakes. Without the character's inner struggles, illness, and drive to satisfy his client, we don't have much invested in the events of the story.

Turn up the "stakes" of the story and watch the audience's interest in the drama increase. Watch us lean into the telling, hanging on your every word. What happens next?

Develop the Arc

This again is to say; your story, despite all the above—stakes, specificity, universality, vulnerability, and simplicity—must have a clear beginning, middle, and end. The world was one way. Something changed all that. And the world is different because of it.

I have a favorite student story by Lara Nuer. While living outside of Montreal, Lara has a very powerful story about her mother's illness when she was a young girl. When she finished telling the very moving narrative, I noticed something unusual about its structure—nearly nothing "happened" in the story.

"My mother was very ill with cancer. Though I was only fifteen years old, I needed to give/deliver her medicine via injection."

The entire arc of Lara's story is this: I had to give my mother a shot, I gave her the shot. She fell asleep.

A microscopic narrative that contains a beginning (I had to give my mother her medicine), a middle (I gave her the shot), and an ending (she fell asleep). However, in the telling of Lara's story, we go through time and space, through Lara's fears of losing her mother, through her fantasy of what life would be like without her, through her mother's joyful interactions with her before her illness, and through the minute details of what it's like for a little girl to find a lymph node and inject her mom with the medicine that could keep her alive another day.

The arc of your story does not have to be complex. It can be the simple action that starts, rises, and completes the narrative while the inner life of the storyteller is explored. Maybe your character gets on a bus, talks to a stranger, and gets off the bus. But the interaction had an impact, the conversation made you reevaluate where you were going, what you were doing, how you were spending your time, money, life...

As with the other aspects and principles that make your story work, a structurally sound spine, regardless of which structure you are using, indicating a beginning, middle, and end will give your audience a satisfying experience and an appreciation of you as the storyteller.

Photo by Kathleen Sheffer, courtesy of The Moth.

Exercise: Assess Your Story Using the "Sticky Story" SUCCESS System

Take a story you are developing and write your own assessment using the following criteria:

Story (Working) Title: _____

Simple—What is the simplest possible summary of the story?

_____

_____

_____

Universal—What universally relatable idea/theme is related in this story? Alternately, what scene, line, or experience in this story could be relatable for anyone who wasn't there?

_____

_____

_____

Concrete—What concrete details or scenes are you, or can you, explicitly describe to build or enhance the color of the story you are telling?

_____

_____

_____

Credible—In what ways are you building credibility for yourself as the storyteller, so the audience can understand and believe this as truth as remembered?

_____

_____

_____

Emotion—What emotions did you feel through this experience? In what ways do you, or can you better, convey those emotions in the telling of the story?

_____

_____

_____

Story—What is the change that you experienced through this story? How is your character different at the end (internally or externally) from how you are at the start?

_____

_____

_____

Surprise—What moment(s) are you building or revealing that will surprise the audience? Alternately, what happens in the story that surprises you when it happens?

_____

_____

_____

Chapter 8

What the Story Is Really About

Before we got married, my wife and I went to premarital couples counseling. We were already engaged and planning our wedding. Our therapist, who for this story I will call Dr. Levy, worked with us to help open "channels of communication" for topics that we were reticent to discuss on our own. We each had fears about "deal-breakers" that we were worried would lead to an argument that might end the relationship if we discussed them.

Rather than answering questions, Dr. Levy offered us "tools" that could be used in our lives and in our relationship going forward. In one session, he compared the process of getting married to feeling like you're on a train. The train is barreling forward, picking up speed. At any time, Dr. Levy instructed us, we can stop the train. We are in control of the train, not the other way around!

That week, my fiancée, Jenny, had a vivid dream that she described to us in our next session. I was driving a car, and she was sitting in the passenger seat. A person came up to her open window and started to attack her. The car wasn't moving, and she was stuck. She couldn't run away, and since I was the driver, she felt powerless. Jenny woke up in a panic from the nightmare.

She did not understand the dream, only that it was full of anxiety. She sensed there was something more going on psychologically. Dr. Levy asked a few questions and Jenny answered about the way she had been feeling with pressure mounting around our wedding—specifically the number of people asking her to make important decisions—about invitations, food, attire, decorations, flowers, and more. She was feeling overwhelmed with all of the decisions coming at her, much like the attacker at the window. She felt trapped, with nowhere to run and nobody to help her.

Dr. Levy instructed her to tell him the dream again after probing with these questions. As she related the details of the attacker and her feelings, she started to put together the connection between her life and how her subconscious imagination was playing it out. As the session concluded, Jenny understood the meaning of this dream; she felt like she was seeing an important encounter playing out in her head and could see herself wrestling with what action to take. Before we stood up to go back home, Dr. Levy said, "Jenny—next time this happens, roll the window up."

Sometimes the answers to the questions we are asking are right in front of us, but we cannot notice them. (Come to think of it, if I'd remembered this moment at the right time, I would not have gotten punched in the face.) This chapter will take a deeper dive into the question "What is your story really about?" Many of our stories are memorable for what happened in them. But to make them really stick in a resonant and impactful way is to find the inner meaning in our stories—its deeper truth or message.

Starting with "Ever Since That Day"

One time, I woke up naked in the hallway of a Holiday Inn.

This is the action at the heart of one of my stories. It's a moment, an incident. So how do I make a story out of it? Is this the beginning of the story? The end? The middle?

The answer is not obvious, so let's explore some more about this event.

Why?

Why was I naked in the hallway? I had sleep-walked from my hotel room, and the door closed behind me, locking me out and waking me up. Sleepwalking was a pattern in my life—I had a history of sleepwalking through my childhood and college years.

What Happened Next?

I felt embarrassed. So, I picked up the newspaper that had been delivered, covered myself, and went to the front desk to get a new key to my room. When the clerk asked me for my ID, I shrugged my shoulders.

How Did I Change Afterward?

I stopped sleeping naked, at least while on this vacation. I did not want to be embarrassed again, so I changed my behavior.

The "ever since that day" of this experience seems to be a behavior change—ever since that day...I stopped sleeping naked. With that information, it's easy to reverse engineer a beginning to this story by flipping the ending.

Once upon a time, I was on vacation in Hawaii. And every day...I slept naked.

This needs some work. Why did you sleep naked? And can you add any (tasteful) color to the experience to help the audience imagine the situation?

(Once upon a time...) I was starting a six-week sabbatical across Southeast Asia. My first stop was Hawaii for my friend's wedding on Oahu. (And every day...) As I was packing a month's gear into a single backpack, I was feeling frugal. I wanted to do as little laundry as possible, so I decided to sleep naked rather than soiling my underclothes. I really don't like sleeping naked. Even while I'm alone, I feel exposed, and don't like the feeling of my body on the rough sheets. (Until one day...) On this first night of the trip, I made the decision to wear nothing to bed. When I woke up, I was standing in the hallway.

Getting better. Starting from where I know I'm ultimately going; I am wrapping the change (sleeping naked to sleeping clothed) around the story spine. Along the way, I am able to add details, character beats, and emotional reactions to make the story come to life.

Take the change in your story, the resolution, and work backward. Find the "everyday" from the "ever since that day" and you have the end of your narrative arc.

Just because this is the arc of the spine, this doesn't mean the story needs to be told in this way. I might jump back in time to another sleepwalking memory, building on the behavior as a pattern rather than an isolated incident. I might try starting the telling of the story at the front desk of the hotel before looping back to the inciting incident. Regardless of how I tell the story, knowing the change will help me get to the bottom of "what is this story really about?"

What Is the Story Really About?

It's definitely not about sleepwalking. Or anything that literally happens in the story. That is the action of the story. Stories are about human behavior, values, or morals. To me, this story is about "feeling exposed," in more than just the physical way. I am starting a six-week sabbatical journey of self-discovery. That journey opens with me, stripped bare and unprotected on the first night, after the first decision I made. To me, then, the story can be evolved to cover more than the jokey feeling of being naked in public—it can speak to a human truth—we are all exposed and alone in the world. And we have to find a way to get through it—alone or with the help of friends or strangers.

Or

Maybe this is a story about being in over your head. I had grown up in the First World, blessed with shelter and security and took for granted the many comforts and conveniences I had. As I was venturing to the Third World, I was given an accidentally unconscious "wake up call" that the world is not all safe. That I need to "cover my own ass" to survive in a world that might have dangers beyond those I'd faced before.

Or

Maybe this is a story about how you don't really know yourself until you've been "exposed" to new experiences.

Any of these, and more, could be distilled from the core events of the story. And the better and deeper I plumb my own story, the richer the telling will become. So, for the time being, I will try working backward from "ever since that day…" to find the arc before pushing into the deeper subconscious truths that lie within.

What Happens in Your Story?

When I am out of my "comfort zone," such as on a vacation, or doing an activity I haven't done before, I feel a heightened state of awareness to the "new." This sense of awareness contrasts with the "everyday" routines that I might be ignoring—driving the same route to work, eating at a nearby taqueria, making my bed in the morning.

When the routine is broken, and everything seems new, or at least I'm noticing things as new, story ideas can start to stack up. An altercation at the ticket counter at the airport—is that a story? Or is that part of a larger "travel" story that also includes helping a sick child on the airplane later that day?

It can be a challenge to set the terminal limits (beginning and end) of a story, so I suggest looking for the shortest, simplest plot of all. Can the story be entirely about the elevator ride up to the hotel room? The time between getting seated and ordering your food on a first date?

By compressing time and action to a simple plot line, you actually free yourself in this breed of storytelling. We're not as limited in what happens, so we open up the possibilities of the inner life, the intrapersonal exchanges, and the contextual epiphanies.

Or

If the story hinges on what happens, and if what happens does so across multiple interactions, exchanges, locations, and scenes, how can we find the simplest version of that? What is the fewest number of scenes, exchanges, interactions, and time jumps needed to communicate the core idea?

When we can simplify, we retain the majority of our audience. When our story jumps and dives, leaps and twists—so does our listener's comprehension, unfortunately.

Have you ever read a chapter of a book only to get to a point where you had to flip back a few pages because though you were reading the words, your mind was drifting? How about the same for a video or movie you were watching? It's right in front of you, but you've missed the plot.

This idea could help to grab that fickle attention span, hold it, and deliver on the promises made in its premise. All before the mind has a moment to wander off.

We over-complicate our messages when we tell short stories. There should be a single simple through line, plot, or concept that our story is telling. If it has a *but* in the middle and a shift to another premise, plot, or meaning, we've written two stories and a bridge to force them together.

Is there a time and place to marry these? Maybe! The test I engage to see if they should overlap is this: is there an even more overarching story or message that connects the two? Or are they separate stories, linked only by a constant:

- They both happened during my time studying abroad

- They both happened while I was dating a specific person

- They both happened while I was recovering from an illness

If there is a greater connector, the "big story" might be:

- Study abroad

- My relationship with this person I dated

- My recovery from being sick

If that is the case, great! You have found the bigger simple story and can link the two stories as episodes in the larger arc of the narrative you are telling. If not, if the two stories are really unique episodes that each have their own beginning, middle, end, message, moral, etc., then I suggest you break them apart. Why dilute the power, message, and emotion of one story by forcing it up against another? You have something greater—two stories from a single time in your life experience that can stand on their own.

Many of us have what we might think of as a major period or turning point/defining moment in our lives. Those times "made us who we are" now, but to take the individual beats or moments apart, we might actually serve our own story better! I think you might unravel the fabric of a complex and important turning point in your own life to find that, like life itself, there is more than one takeaway. More than one lesson that you learned from it. So maybe there is a short series of stories that can stand on their own to illustrate the individual takeaways you got from that experience!

What Really Happens in Your Story?

My dad's brother, my Uncle Bob, died this year. Like any life-cycle event (a birth, graduation, marriage, etc.), a relative dying is a time for reflection about the person who passed and the impact they had on our lives. When I came home for the funeral and we gathered at the cemetery to remember and say farewell to Uncle Bob, stories were told, stories about Uncle Bob's childhood, his growing up, his military service, and his adult life.

Bob lived a life that many in attendance didn't know about. He was in a gang in his youth (The Jesters)! He was an amateur boxer. He loved his kids and he loved his dog, whose ashes were buried with him.

Funerals and eulogies are occasions where we use stories to connect the parts of a person's life together—through the narrative threads that everyone who shares a story provides.

And you know what else happened at Uncle Bob's funeral? Nobody mentioned his widow, who was not invited to the burial. (He died and was cremated several weeks before, without a service, and this was the burial service.) Nobody mentioned her at all. Her life, her relationship, her impact on him, or anything else to do with her. She was absent in every way because she had alienated almost everyone at the event, everyone else who loved Bob as a father, a brother, an uncle, and more.

If I was to develop this into a story—I would be drawn to that detail. The unspoken element, the Achilles heel, the buried secret. The story is of course about Uncle Bob, but to me, it's a story about the complex relationships we have in our lives, the people we love, and the people in their lives who don't like us: the people who try to shut us out, but who cannot stop us from loving someone else.

Every story should ultimately hinge on a single emotion, message, or insight.

That insight is the takeaway that is the root of what your audience will get from your story. You are never just telling an "interesting" story or letting us know more about yourself. That is, to be blunt, uninteresting! Your most interesting story will only be so when I can connect it, your life experience, to myself. I want to hear your most interesting story, and I want to think, "Yes, I know just what you mean. I too am a human and I know now that you are more like me, in a different way, but a way that makes me appreciate you and the choices, situations, and relationships you have experienced."

So often, I meet people and hear their stories, and I think they are convinced that their stories are worth telling because of how *different* and *interesting* they are. And the more I hear them, the more I come back to some fundamental points and principals: I will feel disconnected from or connected to you based on the story.

And when the life experience is far from mine, but I can still connect the human component—the emotion, message, or insight—I feel the best thing that there can be—in love with them. Not love like "love" love. I'm in storytelling love with them. They have made me feel more "me" than I felt before I heard the story.

That's when storytelling is a gift to the audience. It's not about you. It's about us. Give us that, and you have completed the mission.

Does the Plot Support the Meaning?

In class recently, Jeff Hanson told a story about a time when, as a fourteen-year-old, he crashed his grandmother's car. The story has a comic yet relatable premise: a group of classmates, alone at his grandparents' house, wanted some beer. Too afraid to dip into grandpa's beer stash, they decide to take grandma's car to the convenience store to buy some. None of them are old enough to drive or to buy beer, but they have heard this place does not check ID. And one of the boys has completed driver's ed, even if he doesn't yet have his license.

Part one of the mission is a success. They get to the store, acquire the beer, and jubilantly head home. Part two of the mission is a failure.

Pulling into the driveway, in their excitement to share the victory of part one, the driver crashes the car into a telephone pole beside the driveway.

When the party breaks up, Jeff is left alone to lie to his grandparents about the incident. They look deep into his eyes and ask him, "is that what really happened?" He lies again, "yes." "If that's what you say, then I believe you," his grandmother tells the guilt-stricken child.

The story concludes later in Jeff's life, as his own daughter crashes her car, has her own problems with alcohol, and tells him things that, in his heart, he knows are partial, half, or untruths. And he invokes the love that his own grandparents gave him. "If that's what you say, then I believe you."

The plot of this story is very simple: children make two foolish decisions, one a success (buying beer), the other a failure (crashing a car). But the story, clearly, is about neither. This is not a story about buying beer or driving/crashing a car. This is a story about trust, love, friendship, risk, and more.

Up and Down

With every story we develop, we will start with what happened, but to get to the meat of the story, we have to look in two directions— *up* or *down*.

Going Up

When I am listening to or creating a story, I will routinely look for a place where the character is making a big decision, a crisis, or a moment where the character can reflect on the situation they are in before an action is taken, a word is spoken, or a decision is made.

I achieve this by doing what I call "going up." "Going up" is a metaphorical launch out of the story without moving the story forward or backward. It is to leap outside the narrative, as the narrator, and to look upon the moment or incident at play in that moment as if from a helicopter or a kite hovering above. We are looking down at the story with perspective. What is happening here? What am I doing? How does this look from outside the situation? If this was not me, but someone else, what would I advise, consider, or do to assist, prevent, or caution the people involved?

Of course, "going up" is not going to stop the situation at hand. If Jeff had "gone up" before taking grandma's car, none of the trouble would have happened. And none of the fun, either. And this is a story that probably would never have been retold. Jeff might "go up" at any number of places in this particular story, each with a different possible effect on the telling:

- Before taking the car: If Jeff "goes up" before taking the car, he might put into perspective something that we are all thinking, "Wait—I'm too afraid to take grandpa's beer, but not too afraid to steal grandma's car? Sure! Being underage, it's unlikely I'd be able to replace the beer and would have to admit I took it. But with the car, we can get our own beer and get away with it."

- Before the accident: "As we're pulling into the driveway, I'm feeling about as triumphant as a wide receiver who caught the ball in the last second of the big game. I'm a hero to my friends who are jumping up and down on the front lawn, high fiving each other. I'm improvising an end zone dance, whooshing the twelve-pack in a circle in front of me like the football. We had made it home and triumphed over all possible obstacles. Except one." Here we are, creating a frozen moment, freezing the character, and coloring the emotional elation of the experience, all while subtly putting our audience off guard for the shock of what comes next: hitting the telephone pole.

- Before the confession: "When grandma and grandpa walked into the house, they didn't yet know about the car. I felt my face flush and my eyes start to water. Do I do the 'good Catholic Boy' thing and confess my sins? What would I advise myself now, if I was my own friend? I'd say, 'Come clean. They love and trust you. Do not betray that love and trust. They will forgive you.' Or maybe, 'Blame Brian. They never liked him. Say it was his idea and apologize for letting him. Take the responsibility and offer to pay for the repairs.' Instead, I lied." Here, going up can play out multiple sides of the argument. You can be your own devil's advocate and play out different possible outcomes. It's what we would do too. And it sets up the decision's reveal.

Another way I "go up" is to put myself in another person's shoes. When I return to Norman's apartment to clean it out, my audience might remember that I'm about to find his "secret." Instead of rushing to reveal the secret, I "go up" to prolong the moment and to put myself in Norman's shoes.

"So, I'm in his apartment by myself. I let myself in, and I'm cleaning out his apartment and I have that weird moment. I don't know if any of you have ever had to do this thing, it was my first time, where you're there, clearing out the stuff and deciding what to keep, or what to discard, and I'm like 'where are the secrets?'"

"You know, I'm sad, but I'm also alone with somebody else's stuff, and it's making me think about what it would be like in my own house. Like when I go, 'What's the weird narrative that people are going to put together when they see my crap and my six hundred snow globes and my box of random pictures?' All those things that you just

have and amass, and you think, 'this is important.' But none of that is important."

Going Down

If "going up" lifts the storyteller above and out of the narrative for perspective, the other direction worth exploring would be the inverse—"going down" into the inner emotional core of the moment.

Sarah, a student of mine, told a story in class about her past relationship with an older man. It started out like a dream. As Sarah said, "he swept me all the way off my feet." Through the telling of the story, his dark side emerged through taking her money, her self-confidence, her self-worth, and even her physical safety. When she opened up about this to her mother, she was given this gift, "Go to the airport right now. I will pay for you to get on the next plane home." She then continued about the relative value of all the things she lost and the true value of family and friendship.

Structurally speaking, this story was on a "downward spiral." Things were bad. And then they got worse. And then they got worse.

My advice in cases like this—when the heart of the story is a series of examples of all the bad things that happened—is to replace that list by "going down," into the heart of the story. By narrating the emotional toll this is taking, you are cutting to the core of what you are hoping all the examples will lead to.

"I came into this relationship hopeful, innocent, optimistic, and loving. I dreamed of romance, and safety, and companionship for the rest of my life. I didn't mind giving over my bank account information, passwords, and retirement account information for him to reinvest for me. He had my entire trust, his promise of marriage, and knew that he

would do the same for me if I had asked. I had never felt so much trust,
respect, love, and faith in a person as I did with that man."

While I'm alluding to story points here, I am not making them all
scenes (the giving of sensitive information, the wedding proposal). I
am bridging them into my fantasy wish fulfillment scenario.

Then I would cut to the chase. "I didn't see the end coming because
I was looking too hard for the light at the end of the tunnel. By the
time I called my mother, crying, alone, and broken, it was too late.
He didn't just take my savings, my retirement accounts, my identity.
He took the girl that could love and trust and feel and made her
regret ever having done so. As I boarded the plane out of that city
and out of that man's life, I felt something I hadn't felt since the time
I boarded the plane to that city and stepped into it. Hope. Freedom.
Release. Safety."

"Going down" is not just a tactic for heavy subject matter. In lighter
stories, "going down" works just as effectively. A foolish adventure
story is made all the more delightful when we "go down" into the
heart of why we are doing what we are doing. In Jeff's car crash story,
though there's a pensive ending about responsibility and truthfulness,
there are lots of delightful humorous moments of youthful logic.
"Going down" into those can tap into the insecurities and longings he
had as a child.

So, whether you go *up* for perspective or *down* for emotional depth
and empathy, consider these ways to pause the storytelling and offer
the listener a chance for reflection before advancing the narrative.

How Stories Change Over Time

What separates a timely story from a timeless story? Time! When you start down the road of learning storytelling, it becomes readily apparent to you that stories are all around us. The story of our day. The story of our dinner date. The story of putting our child to bed.

Timely stories have a way of articulating our lives as we are living them. They can present, like a diary entry, a situational awareness that can be told with remarkable accuracy and detail, since they are recent experiences.

But take stock of that story and revisit it at a later time—a month, a year, or more—and you will see something else in that story. With time, the story's "ever since that day…" may take on a new shape. You've changed. The situation has changed.

With age, experience, and wisdom, I like to look back at my own stories as dynamic episodes that have the possibility of changing. Sometimes, they work best just as I formed them in the first place. But when I reexamine the stories, I occasionally find some other insight that I can use to modify the experience.

For stories that I am crafting from memory in the first place—a story about a childhood experience or a dramatic one—these are less likely to change. These get more of a sense of a fixed-in-time feeling.

But the ones that are happening now, that are fresh and might lack a bigger perspective, these are ripe to revisit later.

Another time or reason to revisit a story is a situational change that might alter the reception of the story. Say you are a college student and you have a wicked night-out story, full of adventures inspired by terrible, alcohol-infused decision-making. This story might kill when you tell it at a party. But when you come home for Thanksgiving and grandma asks how college is, you might make some changes to the telling of that story.

We have all had mixed life experiences, and to some degree there are events and incidents that we would consider embarrassing, shameful, or inappropriate to discuss in mixed company. "My mother would die if she heard that I told that story!" I am not trying to encourage you to alienate your family and friends by telling a good story, but I think it can be worth the challenge to examine a time in your life, and even a questionable decision or interaction you have had, for the lessons that it may have taught or revealed upon closer examination at a later time.

In other words, you may be sitting on a diamond mine of story material. With shape, perspective, and craft, these memories and experiences which helped define you are prime raw materials for some of the best stories you may have.

One reason is vulnerability. When you open yourself up to showing your fears, worries, and shameful memories, the audience is right there with you.

At a recent *Moth* show, I experienced this firsthand. The theme of the night was "identity." As often happens, many of the would-be storytellers (putting their name in the hat) had come prepared to tell a story. But one man arrived at the show and, upon seeing the theme posted, was reminded of his own story and, taking a chance, put his name in the hat.

When I drew his name, the man, in his mid-fifties with salt and pepper hair and a bushy moustache, made his way to the stage, his face already a bit flush. "I can't believe I got picked," he muttered, then further explaining himself, "I have never told this story to anyone before. It happened a long time ago. My two daughters are here in the audience, as is one of their boyfriends and his mother!"

The whole audience craned their necks to see the faces of his family and friends, all sitting in the center section, midway back. The daughters were in their late teens, prime embarrassment age, and to be with their boyfriends and extended families? The stage was set; the stakes were already high. What could this "never told" story be?

With high expectations, I was not disappointed. The man had worked as a writer for a college-oriented travel ratings book while attending college. While many students get choice assignments in Tuscany or romantic Greek Islands, this guy was assigned Death Valley, California. In the middle of the summer. After visiting the handful of restaurants, motels, and landmarks, he was bored and decided to visit a brothel at the edge of town.

As he revealed this detail, you could see his daughters shrink down in their seats a few inches. Their dad pressed on, but notably, in the most graceful and tactful way. This was not a story of sexual conquest or the wild times he had in his youth; this was a story of his embarrassment, told with equal embarrassment. It's a sensitive subject, but the storyteller had us curious what would happen.

As he moved from the entrance to a bedroom with a worker there, the young woman recognized him—they had gone to high school together! Here he was, trying to escape from his world, only to be thrust face-first into the heart of his fears. He grew up, went to medical school, and became what we would call a "grown up," but his checkered past rested inside him. We all carry secrets and you never know what secrets the person next to you harbors.

Amusingly, after relating this story, another woman in the audience remembered him. She also worked for the same publisher, at the same time. To me, it was a great tactful repurposing of a personal story that could update with the times.

Exercise: "Go Up and Go Down"

Take a story you are developing and explore "going up" and "going down."

Story summary—What is the story about?

_____

_____

_____

_____

_____

_____

Going up—What is really happening in this situation? What perspective can you put on the events with the benefit of hindsight? Alternately, in the moment, what musings, decisions, or opposing ideas did you experience that helped shape the decisions you made at the time?

_____

_____

_____

_____

_____

_____

Going down—At what point(s) in your story can you pause the telling to deepen the emotion? Where can we stop the forward action to focus on who you are, how you react in situations like this, and build interest, curiosity, or understanding for how you will ultimately react or act?

_____

_____

_____

_____

_____

_____

What is your story really about? In light of the "ups" and "downs" explored, what is the bigger idea/theme/message that your story is showing or telling us?

_____

_____

_____

_____

_____

_____

_____

Chapter 9

Remembering Your Story

This chapter is based on the ways I have practiced remembering and telling my stories for performance. It's a technique I have developed over many years and then, researching the history of oratory, have enhanced to give the storyteller the confidence to tell their story while also the freedom to connect with the audience and experience "in the moment" presence.

Memory Techniques for Storytellers

In ancient Rome, and popularized during the Middle Ages and Renaissance periods, orators were taught from a book called *Rhetorica ad Herennium* the art of public speaking. Bringing the craft from the political sphere to the people, this book has survived to our times and contains, among other interesting elements, the first known system for mnemonic memorization.

It is this system, or a system based upon it, that I have adopted for storytellers to use in performance. The strategy is based on the concept that you *know* your story. You lived it, you developed it, and you inherently can relate the detailed contents of that story to an audience. With the inherent knowledge, I apply mnemonic memorization systems to recall the sequence of my story, so it can be recalled effectively as desired.

The strategy for this kind of memorization hinges on our innate abilities to recall images more easily than words. One of the most common traits I have observed with storytellers awaiting their story at a storytelling show is that person avidly poring over a three- or four-page printout of their story in essay form, "cramming" it into their head like a student reviewing notes before an exam. They've written their story out and, reaching the stage, attempt to retell it with the eloquence and literary flair of how they'd written it.

And the trouble with this method of storytelling? We can tell. We can tell when someone is telling us a story and when someone is reading us a story or reciting a memorized essay. I would generally prefer, in this situation, to have the person read me their essay to do their writing justice and to convey the wording as they intended it. I enjoy reading, and I enjoy attending author events where the writer reads from their own work. It's nice to see their craft and to appreciate the way they construct it.

I'm not expecting, in those cases, the author to paraphrase the story, the details, or the dialogue. I'm expecting it to be read in their "voice" as an author.

At a storytelling event, just as with a conversation you might have with a friend, the style tends to skew less formal, less rhetorical, and less scripted. Generally, the voice of the storyteller is a version of their own. Their storytelling voice opens and reveals their experience as lived, as experienced, and as remembered.

Can that voice contain practiced, rehearsed, and scripted aspects? Of course! I appreciate a storyteller who can weave a narrative and carry me on its words, phrases, and narrative energies through the experience to a satisfying conclusion.

But…

When the storytelling stops being a story-told, and starts to feel like a script-performed, the storyteller loses their credibility. Their over-rehearsed, or perhaps under-rehearsed, performance of the story can do a disservice to the story itself. When I feel I am being delivered a monologue versus a story, I evaluate the words as if I were hearing a staged reading of a book or a play. I lose the personal connection to the storyteller.

So…

Here is the ad Herennium-based system for memorizing your way through the story without falling into a trap of rote memorization and losing the spontaneity of the story in its telling:

- Break the Story into BEATS

- Connect the BEATS to HOOKS

- Fluidly RECALL the story by recalling the connected visual memories

Beats

There are many ways to conceive of a beat for a story. A beat may be a scene, a sequence, or a specific detail in the telling of the story. For a shorter story, such as Jack and Jill, the beats could be broken out as:

1. Jack and Jill (once upon a time)

2. Went Up the Hill (and every day)

3. To fetch a pail of water (until one day)

4. Jack fell down (because of that)

5. And broke his crown (because of that)

6. Jill came tumbling after (until finally)

For a longer story, such as my Cousin Norman story, the beats may be more random—though indicative of what is or will happen through the telling of the story. Here are the beats I use for this story:

1. Norman Dies

2. Tying Up Loose Ends

3. Discovering the Secret

4. Describing Norman

5. The Movie *Seven*

6. Budget Travel

7. *The A**hole Monologues*

8. The Birthday Party

9. Cleaning Norman's apartment

10. The Will

Both of these examples give a succinct and not too verbose summation of the beats of the stories. In one (Jack and Jill), the beats are the same as the story points—though there is a lot left to the imagination. In the second (Norman), the beats are groupings of scenes that help to keep the storyteller on track to deliver the key information without losing the plot.

Connecting Beats to Hooks

In order to recall the beats of these stories, I'm going to try two separate "storage systems." The storage systems are what can be referred to as hooks—containers to hold the story so that, in your mind as you tell it, you can clearly and rapidly recall the beats.

Nearly anything could be a hook. Your own body has a logical sequence—feet, knees, legs, hips, butt, etc. Your hand has a sequence—thumb to pinky, left and right. Your house, your car, your office, your classroom…each might have a clear and distinct sequence that you could use to create a sequential storage system.

It is important that the storage hooks be specific for you—your own body, your own classroom, your own home. You must be able to clearly visualize it for this memory technique to work. So, if it's your home, picture the sequence—maybe it's the front steps, the doorknob, the coat rack in the foyer, the hall bathroom, the kitchen counter—of specific landmarks along the way.

Hooks

1. Toes

2. Knees

3. Your Butt

4. Your Heart

5. Your Mouth

6. Your Brain

To each of these hooks we will now connect exactly one beat of the story by converting the beat to a visual image that can give me a clear and vivid recall of the story moment.

Images

1. Jack and Jill—Picture a jackhammer

2. Went up the hill—Picture a green mossy hill

3. To fetch a pail of water—Picture a rusty bucket of water

4. Jack fell down—Picture a tree with beautiful fall colors

5. And broke his crown—Picture a broken tooth crown

6. And Jill came tumbling after—Picture a girl tumbling in a clothes dryer

Putting Them Together

Create a mental picture of each:

1. JACKHAMMERING your own toes

2. BIG GREEN MOSSY HILLS growing out of your knees

3. SITTING YOUR BUTT in a rusty bucket of ice water

4. A BEAUTIFUL FALL-COLORED TREE growing out of your heart/chest

5. FEELING THE PAIN of a broken crown on your tooth

6. IMAGINING A GIRL TUMBLING as if in a dryer, inside your skull

The examples I chose are, intentionally, quick graphic, vivid, and even violent or disturbing (Jackhammering my own toes?!). By describing the images you select in an outrageous situation, they come to mind more vividly. So you might or might not remember an object like a jackhammer, but it is easier to remember if the jackhammer is crushing your toes. The painful concept of a JACKHAMMER demolishing my own TOES is a sticky, emotional, and specific one that is easy to recall. Ow! I see/feel a jackhammer crushing my toes (in my mind). Jack! That's the first beat of my story.

Next up—Green Mossy Hills on my Knees. And on and on until I have gone through my body-checklist and captured the story in a visual and physical checklist. I imagine myself walking on stage, *wearing* my story like an invisible suit of armor. No one but me can see or feel it, but I know my story because it is physically attached to my person.

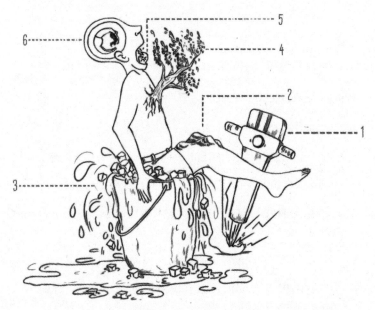

A disturbing imaging of what my mental map might actually look like to translate "Jack and Jill" into six story beats.

For my Norman story, I will use a different storage concept—the fingers on my two hands. This works out well for this story since it has ten beats and I have ten fingers.

Hooks

1. Right Thumb

2. Right Index

3. Right Middle

4. Right Ring

5. Right Pinky

6. Left Thumb

7. Etc.

Images

1. Norman Dies—Picture a Tombstone

2. Tying Up Loose Ends—Picture a Bow Tie

3. Discovering the Secret—Picture a mouth zipped closed (holding a secret)

4. Describing Norman—Picture a huge nose (like the one I will describe)

5. The Movie *Seven*—Picture dark sunglasses (part of that story)

6. Budget Travel—Picture a coin

7. The A**hole Monologues—Picture a butt

8. The Birthday Party—Picture a burning birthday candle

9. Cleaning Norman's apartment—Picture a broom

10. The Will—Picture an old-fashioned rolled up parchment

Putting Them Together

Create a mental picture of each:

1. TOMBSTONE sticking out of Right Thumb

2. BOW TIE around Right Index Finger

3. ZIPPER running up the length of Right Middle Finger

4. HUGE NOSE growing out of Right Ring Finger

5. DARK SUNGLASSES on Right Pinky Finger

6. COIN spinning on Left Pinky

7. HUMAN BUTT growing on Left Ring Finger

8. BURNING CANDLE dripping wax on Left Middle Finger

9. BROOM sticking out of Left Index Finger

10. ROLLED PARCHMENT sticking out of Left Thumb

Again, a bit of an obscure collection of images, but with some repetitive practice of just these ten beats and images connected to my ten fingers, I am able to walk on stage with my hands full of my story. I look down at my fingers and, in my mind's eye, "see" a tombstone sticking out of my thumb and knew my story will start with Norman dying. And on deck, a bow tie—cuing me that I'm going to talk about "tying up loose ends" next.

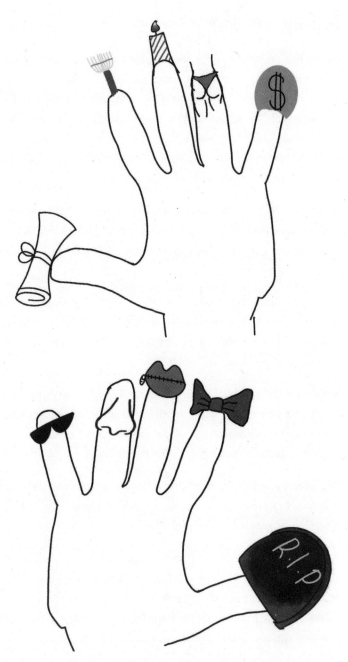

My mental map of the "Norman" Story, seen only by me in my mind when telling the story.

Telling the Story

Fluidly RECALL the story by recalling the connected visual memories. While this sounds crazy, my actual process while telling a story, "banked" in this way, is to fluctuate between looking at (physically, or mentally) each "hook" to recall the beat in question—and then to shift my attention to the audience or to the story at hand. As I relate and recall that beat of the story, I gradually "peek" up the story spine to the next "hook" to remind myself what is coming.

So, for my hands, I would look down and, seeing the zipper running up the middle of the finger, I am veering my telling toward the story beat that is hooked there—"And that's where I discovered that Norman had a secret."

Now I look ahead and see the huge NOSE on my next finger, so I say, "Let me tell you a little bit about Norman first…" Finger by finger, or hook by hook, I stay right on track with the telling of my tale, without fear that I will get "lost" as I tell it.

Will I potentially "forget" to include a part of my story? A line that I really like, or a specific way I usually describe it? Yes. And to me, that's fine! As long as the meat and potatoes of my story and my storytelling remains intact, I consider it a success.

And when I recall what I missed, and if it merits its own beat to be not forgotten, I can re-create my hooks and add that beat right in there, so it is not forgotten the next time I tell the story.

This system, of course, relies heavily on your openness, and ability, to "color and advance" as you go! If the beats are the "advance" markers, what you do in between is your coloring muscle flexing for all its worth. Color with details. Color with side stories. Color with emotion. And then ride on back to the beat-map and proceed.

Another advantage this system can have is for timed shows like *The Moth*, which limits stories told to under six minutes. At five minutes, a sound or musical note is played, letting the storyteller know they should wrap up their story. With a beat-map of this kind, you can opt to directly limit your "color" in this part of (usually the end of) the story and get to the conclusion before the six-minute music or sound is played.

While this might seem "hard" or "impossible" to fathom, believe me when I say that your visual memory is better than you know if you haven't experienced it. Images, especially if you make them vivid, specific, and detailed, are very sticky—stickier than words, phrases, and descriptions. You will always know where you are and where you are going when you try this memory technique. It's worked for thousands of years!

Exercise: Create a Mental Map

Take ten items around your room and attach them to your:

1. Toes

2. Knees

3. Thigh/Leg

4. Butt

5. Love handle

6. Belly

7. Heart

8. Chin

9. Forehead

10. Top of your head

Create a strong visual connection localized at that hook to sink it into memory. See it. *Feel it.* Let it make your laugh. Then, move on until you have the whole map built.

Then, recall them, in order, one by one.

For bonus points, set a timer for, say, an hour, or a day from now—and see if you can recall this list of ten things!

Exercise: Create a Mental Map of a Story

Take a story you are working on or a completed story you know well. Alternately, take a well-known story that you can try breaking into beats (fairy tales work well). Map the story using the guidelines taught in this chapter:

Hooks

Allocate the following body parts as the "hooks" you will use to store your story, in this order:

1. Feet

2. Knees

3. Thigh Muscle

4. Butt

5. Love Handle

6. Belly

7. Heart

8. Mouth

9. Nose

10. Top of your Head

Make any adjustments if you would like to substitute a body part but commit to remembering this sequence and review it without looking at the list.

Beats

Break your story into no more than ten beats with a simple one-to-four-word phrase that will recall where in the story you are going (example: the box, pizza, roommates come home, return address, etc.).

1. _____

2. _____

3. _____

4. _____

5. _____

6. _____

7. _____

8. _____

9. _____

10. _____

Attach images for each beat to each hook, in order. For example, "feet are crushing a cardboard box," "oozing mozzarella cheese and pepperonis in place of the skin on my knees," etc. Don't be afraid to be gross, violent, or ridiculous. You are more likely to remember the images the more specific, visual, and graphic they are.

1. _____

2. _____

3. _____

4. _____

5. _____

6. _____

7. _____

8. _____

9. _____

10. _____

Picture each of these images on each of the hooks in sequence. Just focus on the images in sequence and run through the list several times, making adjustments as needed to make each image "sticky" to the hooks, one through ten.

Now, tell yourself (or someone else) the story, focusing as you do on each successive image/hook combination as you progress through the story. If you have nobody available, set up a recording device, such as your phone or computer, and tell the story that way.

Chapter 10

Beginning and Ending

The most important part of your story, as far as I am concerned, is the way it starts and ends. Period. Nail those beats and the rest is cake.

Sounds easy, right? It can be, if you make it a priority in the rehearsing and telling of your story!

Without it, this is how most stories start:

"So…um…(Sigh)…ok…wow, I'm really nervous… So…this is a little bit complicated but…ok. I was…twenty years old. Yeah, 1990…yeah. I was twenty years old…"

Not exaggerating. This is all too common. You try to wing it and you go up on stage and start a story like this? You have lost in so many ways. You've lost our attention. You've lost our confidence that this will be a good story. You've lost time (for a timed storytelling competition). The rest of the time, even if this is an amazing thing that happened to you, is spent making up for this rocky beginning.

Open Strong

The way you start your story sets the tone for the experience we are about to have. Are you confident? Nervous? Direct or indirect? And as for the narrative—are you creating a reason for me to stay interested in the story?

Crafting a strong opening line or paragraph for your story can create so many positive emotions. Curiosity about what will happen! Tone for the story to come! An introduction to you as the narrator!

What's more, if you are a nervous presenter, knowing with confidence the specific words you will say as soon as you reach the stage gives you a focus and can be a sure-fire way to allay those nerves. Start clean and strong and give yourself, and your story, an immediate boost. Open your story with the words that you have planned and wanted to say and feel yourself relax. Yeah! I did it. Now I set to work telling the rest of the story.

The other cardinal sin when starting a story is to give it a really, really, really, really, really long on-ramp, a complicated and convoluted backstory that is, basically, unimportant to the story you are telling. I call it storytelling calisthenics. You work yourself up to the story by stalling the story itself because, for you, this was the interesting and important backstory that led to the events in question.

When in reality, as a story, we can come in *much* later and feel fully present and interested in your story's world without all the background about how many brothers and sisters you had and what your dad did for a living.

The story is about your experience. If any of that backstory is important to the story, find a place to work it in when we need it. Few things pin a storyteller as amateurish and unprepared as a rambling, unstructured opening.

Except

Remember the doctor who did not plan to come up on stage? Who came to a show not prepared to tell a story, but came on stage and told a story he had never told before?

The opening of his story was about as unstructured, unprepared, and unplanned as you can imagine. He was mortified. He was shaking. He made a minute's worth of excuses before he started the story. And he had us all in the palm of his hand! Because he was so vulnerable, so open, so exposed, the audience fell in love with him and gave him latitude to wander into the story.

And when the story actually began, we were sitting on the edge of our seats, thrilled to discover what long-buried secret would be revealed.

So, it's not a system without exception, which is for certain. But for the most part, if you are looking to craft a story from a life experience, let's treat the doctor's example as the exception and not the rule. Go out with nothing planned and it's possible you will stumble into a good or even a great story.

It's possible you will not! And that's good! It's what we do all the time, brainstorming and making discoveries in the moment. Build on what does work to improve on the parts that don't.

With a top-notch opening line, that gets our interest and attention, you set the snowball down the mountain with confidence and grace that can establish our curiosity for the story you are about to tell.

Stick the Landing

Equally if not more important to a strong opening line is your closing. Leave the audience on a strong line, and they are far more likely to like, remember, and appreciate your story.

A strong ending can actually perform a miracle. It's not uncommon for a story to get "soft" in the center. To have moments that do not land quite as well as others. But when the ending comes together and leaves the audience with a strong, emotionally satisfying experience, all is forgiven.

One of the local Bay Area masters of the craft of the last line is Eva Schlesinger.

With her quirky, deadpan delivery and tightly scripted stories, Eva's storytelling style is, essentially, the opposite approach to most of what I teach in this book. She knows her stories word for word and delivers them with high-pitched precision.

And it's not for everyone. This overly scripted approach can put off some of the audience. She occasionally loses credibility for her perfection—can this really be a true story? But when she lands the punch line at the end, no matter what the audience thought of the story as it was unfolding, they laugh, cheer, and admire her skill.

One of her recent stories involved a can of inexpensive coconut water. The plot of the story centered on the mechanics of getting the included straw into the beverage container where the price tag gets inadvertently in the way. It's a relatively odd and specifically unexciting premise for a story, yet the way she obsesses over the details and the mechanics of getting a sip of the refreshment leaves the audience feeling bewildered and amused.

As the story places its emphasis on this detail, and the narrator's singular focus on it, the story takes a turn from the absurd to the ridiculous. And then the punch line arrives: "Some price tags are difficult to swallow. This one went down easily."

In a single line, she sums up the theme, message, and drama of the story. You can't ask for much more than that.

So How Do You End Your Story?

When crafting an ending, my favorite place to look is backward. What have we already established, introduced, and set up? Is there something that can be reincorporated? A line? A piece of advice you received?

We will come into your story "clean." We have little or no knowledge about you, your life, and your experience. Everything we know, we are learning from you. With this in mind, you have the power to direct our knowledge and understanding of you. And you set us up for the ending. So, lay in clues, motifs, and imagery that hold us through to the end. And when you succinctly leave us with that, with a memory, a message—you win a piece of our hearts.

Another way to find your ending is to start with it. If you know where you want your story to end—the punch line, the shocking conclusion, and the lesson—then you can build the story backward! Remember our story spine and the connection between "everyday" and "ever since that day." If you know the end of your story's "ever since that day" then build up to that and reverse engineer the beginning to prepare us for that conclusion.

Here is an example. Randy Beard tells this great story in need of an ending. He begins with,

"I have two childhood memories of my mother. The first, I'm about three years old, playing with her typewriter, and I get in trouble. The second, I'm walking with her to pick up my brother from church. I'm five years old. It's dusk and we live less than a mile from the church. I remember the white line on the road next to me, my mom's hand in mine on my left side, and the headlights of a car behind us... Then I remember feeling the wind getting knocked out of me, like I was punched in the stomach..."

In the story, Randy recounts the confusing aftermath of the car accident, which ultimately reveals that his mother died that night. Dealing with the tragic aftermath of the incident, Randy is left with lingering, unanswered questions—people that don't believe he too was hit by the car—after all, wouldn't a five-year-old have died if he was hit by the same car that killed his mom? But the lingering sense memory of getting "punched in the stomach" stays with him. Until one day, telling the story to a girlfriend, she suggests, "did you ever consider that was your mother pushing you out of the way?"

He reconsiders the details of the memory—that when he came to, he was lying in "the middle of the road" while police lights flashed all around.

And then, Randy says, "but I don't know how to end my story."

How Would You End This?

The fruits of a good ending are usually born of seeds you planted early in the story. Sometimes they are hard to notice. In Randy's case, I think they are right there for the plucking.

Look at his opening line, "I have two childhood memories of my mother..." This is a perfect opportunity to use this phrasing as a refrain with added impact, with a twist.

Here is how I would end this story, bringing back the phrasing from the opening, with one major change:

"I have two childhood memories of my mother. The first, I'm about three years old, playing with her typewriter, and I get in trouble. The second, is when my mother saved my life."

Repeating a phrase, a line, a word—or bringing an idea back from somewhere else early in the story gives us the full-circle experience. Together we remember where we started, where we've been, and where we are now.

Give your audience a final uplift, a swell of emotion, or a laugh, and you have a winner on your hands. What's more, by closing a story with this emotional beat, we will forgive the parts that perhaps were not quite as strong, funny, interesting, or concrete.

Start strong and stick the landing and you have the makings of a winning story.

Exercise: String of Pearls

String of pearls is a great group exercise to play with the construction of a story's beats, specifically its beginning and ending.

To play, the group self-selects their place in the order of the game—going in when they have a hit but playing one at a time.

The goal is to tell a complete story, one line at a time, but out of sequence.

The first player will go to either the far (audience) left side of the playing area or "stage" and say the first line of a made-up story.

Then a second person will go to the other extreme (far right side) and say the last line, trying as much as possible to make it as disconnected or unrelated to the first line. Then the "entire story" is retold. In other words, the "first line" is re-said (exactly as it was the first time), followed by the "last line."

Then, one at a time, the rest of the players each fill in a line of the story wherever they can, any place in the line, bringing things together and ending up with a story that makes complete sense.

Every time a new line is added, the players go down the string and repeat their lines first to last. The fun of the game, though, is that these lines can be told in any order. So, the third player will be "somewhere" in the middle of the story—but the fourth player can decide if their line will go between the first and the middle or the middle and the end. On and on, the lines are added, with the "entire story" (in progress) is retold with the addition of each line.

The subsequent players, then, are increasingly looking to help "connect the dots." Seeing a setup in one place and paying it off later. Or vice versa, seeing something that happens later and introducing it earlier in the story, so that the entire narrative makes sense when the final player enters the scene. Each player must find a gap and fill it. Or, to clarify something that is vague or undefined in the story. Or just to say the first thing that pops into their head.

For reluctant groups, I remind them that the sooner they "get in" the story, the easier it is (as there's less logic to reincorporate). The last player tends to be the "cleanup" batter—adding the glue that holds any disjointed or unresolved matters together.

This game works best with seven or eight players but can be played with more (even many more!). It can also be played with as few as three for a basic story that has a beginning, middle, and end.

When broken apart in this way, it's fun and interesting to see how the components of a story relate to and support each other, and how your story is built and wrapped by the first and last lines. Make sure to listen carefully to what has already been said and not to reject or ignore these offers. As every line counts, it helps to make each new sentence as detailed as possible.

The "string of pearls" is complete when all players are in the line and the entire story is told from beginning to end.

This can also work as a writing exercise where story elements are written on Post-it notes or note cards tacked to a board or taped to the wall, with each participant or student adding one to each story until all stories are complete.

The Last Thing to Do Before You Tell Your Story

Let's put it all together now. You have an opening line and a closing line. You have a beat-by-beat plan for your story mapped in some mental checklist. But it's time to go on stage and tell your story.

How do you put this all together in a cohesive package? I have a trick I use to give myself a mental "warm-up" right before I get on stage.

I say the "opening" and "closing" lines out loud, to myself.

If I was Randy, directly before getting on stage, I'd say out loud, "I have two childhood memories of my mother," and, "I have two childhood memories of my mother."

Yes, they are the same line. That's just how Randy's story is. For a story with different first and last lines, I'd say those. Like, "This is a story about my cousin Norman, Norman Wiener," and "I miss him."

With these two lines in my head and in my "mouth," physically, I am far more likely to speak them, articulately, when I reach the stage. Nervous or not, I give myself that little boost of confidence that I can say the two *most important lines* of my whole story the way I want them to sound.

So, I reach the microphone, take a breath, and say my opening line. In my head, subconsciously, I am over the first hurdle! I did it! First line—*DONE*. And they didn't boo me off that stage!

Now that the hardest part is behind me, I set out, hook by hook, beat by beat, through the story. Somewhere through the telling of the story, I get that sense that I'm reaching the ending. Either I'm running short on time, or I'm actually approaching the end of the story.

Whether it went as well as I planned or practiced, or not, I start to "look ahead," with a mental recall to my "last line."

Without rushing to it, I have it ready, and prepared, I deliver it with finality and confidence.

Think about how much better a confidently delivered closing line would sound compared to the "typical" story that kind of runs out of gas at the end. "I guess that's it?" I've heard these actual words spoken countless times in shows. Or some variation of them, including, "That's it," "I guess that's the end," and, "Um, and a bunch of other stuff happened after, but I'm out of time, bye."

Stick that ending and you leave us appreciating you, and your story.

Another advantage to the strategies I am describing is to focus your energy as you wait to tell your story. A common practice at storytelling shows is for the storyteller to sit, waiting to tell their story, with a printed copy of the story nervously held in the storyteller's hands. Folded and unfolded, over and over, skimmed and scanned, the storyteller "crams" the story in their head, hoping that when they reach the microphone, like facts memorized for a history exam, their story will "come back to them."

I do not subscribe to this strategy! Cramming your story in the moments leading up to your story is more likely to add to your anxiety. Storytellers who are married to or anxious about forgetting a part of their story are more likely to forget a part of their story and to feel that tinge of "darn," when they realize they've missed, forgotten, or incorrectly stated something from how it was so beautifully written on their cheat sheet.

By focusing that early energy instead on just your opening and closing lines, and repeating those lines, you will know that your story will start and end strong. What happens in between *should* come out fine. It's a true story, after all, one you lived and should be able to relate without notes, a script, or a plan of any kind. Having planned ahead will make it better, of course—the sequence, the attention to concrete detail and the interweaving of plot and description…but when it's time to shine, I feel it's better to be relaxed, present, and to crush those first and last lines.

One of my favorite experiences of this technique in action happened at the beautiful Castro Theater in San Francisco on the occasion of the second-ever San Francisco *Moth GrandSLAM* competition. The GrandSLAM is a large event produced by *The Moth* for winners of the smaller monthly StorySLAMs. Only winning storytellers are invited to perform, rather than the other format, where storytellers are selected from a hat. The audience is many times larger than a typical StorySLAM. In San Francisco, the venue holds close to 1,400 people! Even the most comfortable performers would have a "gulp" moment standing on a Broadway-sized stage, staring across that many faces eager to listen to your story.

On this occasion, my friend and former student Dave Mahony had won a Slam and was called up (by me) to tell his story. Dave walked up the wooden stairs and across the stage, past the red velvet curtain that stretched as high as the ornate proscenium ringing the stage. Striding forward, Dave stopped center stage and, rather than approaching the microphone, turned his BACK to the audience. Facing the curtain instead of the audience, I saw Dave speak, out loud, to himself, the first and last lines of his story!

Then, Dave calmly turned around, took two steps forward and spoke his first line, flawlessly, into the mic.

Dave took that moment for himself. It lasted maybe ten seconds. Ask anyone in the audience that night if they remember it, and I doubt anyone would. It was over as soon as it started. But it gave Dave the boost of confidence in his own story at the time that he needed it.

If anyone from the audience *had* noticed it, as 1,400 people were watching Dave, it's likely they were intrigued, curious what was happening. Here was the next storyteller on stage *not* telling his story. What's happening? Then, he turns and starts his story. Crisis resolved. Show saved.

Taking that moment for himself, Dave gave himself the lift he had practiced and was happy with the way his story was told. The stage is yours when you are telling your story. Taking your time by giving yourself a moment to center yourself is totally your right and your choice, should you want it.

Having a clear, defined, and well-planned closing line, and saying it with confidence, indicates to your audience that you are in control of the storytelling. You land that last line, and the audience feels it, knows it, and appreciates you for it.

I have a story that takes place when I was twenty-five years old. Here are the first and last lines I use to tell this story:

First Line: The box was waiting on my doorstep when I came home.

Last Line: When you find a box, open it.

The rest of the story, as you might have guessed, is the story of that box. My lines aren't too complicated or too hard to remember. But as I walk on stage to tell them, I say them out loud. "The box was waiting on my doorstep when I came home. When you find a box, open it."

In a recent event at *StorySLAM Oakland*, I received a rather elaborate introduction from the host of the show, Julie Soller. When I arrived on stage, it would have been strange to launch right into my story without acknowledging the introduction, so I thanked the host, and gave her a kind of "reverse" introduction—telling a short story about her! Then, I took a moment, a breath, and said, "The box was waiting on my doorstep when I came home."

It was clear to all that the "story" had begun because I started it with purpose.

This Is the Secret

Be purposeful, clear, and confident, and the audience will lean right into you and hang on the words you are telling. You want to grab them early, hold them, and release them with the last line.

Exercise: Beginnings and Endings

Brainstorm possible first and last lines for your story.

Don't be precious. They may not be perfect, but see if you can set intrigue with the start and satisfy or pay off with the closing:

Story Title:

_____

_____

_____

FIRST LINE IDEAS

_____

_____

_____

_____

_____

_____

_____

_____

_____

_____

LAST LINE IDEAS

_____

_____

_____

_____

_____

_____

_____

_____

_____

_____

_____

_____

_____

_____

_____

_____

_____

_____

Chapter 11

Storytelling Shows

Now that you have a story or two practiced and prepared, it's time to tackle that bucket list item and get yourself on stage at a show and tell it. Like the craft of developing a story, it's a good idea to be kind to yourself when that moment comes. Your first time up on stage may not be perfect! You may forget parts of your story, lose your place, or draw a complete blank.

Regardless of the venue, audience, and tone of the event, most audiences for true stories tend to give the performers the benefit of the doubt. This is not stand-up comedy, where the audience has a typically high expectation that you will make them laugh. And when you don't, they may feel confident enough to heckle you!

Storytelling does not usually draw hecklers. It tends to draw humans who have lived lives and who are there to listen and support people brave enough to stand up and tell their true stories in public. So, they can feel connected, entertained, and moved by others' stories.

This chapter will break down the most common types or varieties of storytelling shows, including what to expect and how to prepare for each one. It will also offer some performance tips and tricks that may come in handy for performers, seasoned or not. Finally, it will offer some ideas and advice for how to plan, produce, and promote your own storytelling shows!

Types of Storytelling Shows

Most storytelling shows come in one of two formats—or a combination of the two. "Hat Draw" is an open-mic style format. "Curated" shows have the performers selected in advance.

Hat Draw

Shows like *The Moth StorySLAM* are set up as open-mic style "hat draws." The performers are selected from the paying audience by a host or producer, one at a time. Similar to a classic coffeehouse "open mic," the producers seldom if ever know what the stories are going to be, so it's common at these kinds of events for there to be some kind of stated or published guidelines for what is expected, welcomed, or deemed appropriate for the stage.

A *truly* open mic is likely to draw a grab bag of performance styles ranging from music acts, stand-up comedy, storytelling, and general "variety" formats including classic vaudeville staples like ventriloquism, puppetry, and magic!

By limiting or defining the content, a hat draw storytelling show will generally declare certain parameters to create a consistent flow to the event as a whole, including the following:

Time

Typically, a time limit is set per act. This is done to keep the show on track and to allow for a relatively "fair" amount of stage time for each performer. The time can range from short (five minutes) to longer (over twenty minutes) and usually depends on the total number of planned performers for the event.

Topics

While not always the case, many hat draw shows set a "theme" or topic as an organizing concept for the event. The topics are often, but not always, set to allow a relatively broad interpretation to allow for a diverse range of stories and points of view within the show. Have a highly specific topic like "fifth grade teachers," might inspire some and stymie others. "Teachers" or "education," on the other hand, can allow for a broader definition or interpretation and hence lead to surprising stories, different kinds of teachers (Sunday school, driver's ed, that older cousin who taught you about "cool" music) or different definitions of education (sorority initiation, cheating on a drug test, learning to trust your own instincts…).

Tone

Most shows consider the audience they are appealing to and set or suggest a tone for the stories. Some shows may look to cater to mature, erotic, or overtly "adult" or taboo subject matter and will usually indicate as such in their marketing, choice of venue, or in the way the event is staged. Similarly, a kids' show or business-oriented tone, such as you might see at an industry-specific conference or retreat, would take on a more controlled or PG-rated tone.

Truth

Not all shows are the same. Some welcome a range of story content (including music acts, group acts, and improvisation). Another aspect that is often defined at a storytelling show is whether the stories are expected to be true. Many shows welcome fiction. Others limit the content to true stories, or at least true "as remembered."

Text

Another variable for shows is their policy toward reading your story versus performing without notes, prompters, or cues.

Type

Finally, most shows will limit or otherwise define what types of content is expected or accepted on their stage. I have been a storyteller at many events that welcome dance, instrumental music, and improv as a part of the variety of performances encouraged in the evening while also organizing the evening around a theme.

Hat draw events also tend to define their own protocols of how participants are selected. Some take advance submissions and notify participants ahead of time. Others collect interest on site and set an order, such as first-come-first-up. Still others collect interested parties and wait to select the next performer until the previous act is finished.

Hat draw formats have advantages and disadvantages. On the positive side, by not limiting or curating the content, except by the defined parameters, if any, you are likely to draw an enthusiastic and diverse audience of curiosity seekers and storytellers alike. The variety of stories I hear in an evening at *The Moth* can be outright life-affirming. Seeing as wide a range of ages, races, and genders sharing one stage to tell stories of their unique life experiences can be so uplifting. And it would be a challenge for most producers to curate as wide a range of stories as might be found at a StorySLAM. The full spectrum of experiences and levels of experience in storytelling can also be quite interesting and educational. There is a real delight to be found in watching a nervous storyteller who's never been on stage before make an audience laugh, cry, or break into applause.

Among the disadvantages of a hat draw show, is the fact that, as a performer, you are often not guaranteed a spot in the lineup. For a slam-type format, where you may not get on stage, it's better to attend only if you consider yourself, in addition to a storyteller, a fan of the form! I like to attend these kinds of shows as an audience member first, considering it "nice" or "unexpected" to be selected to tell my story on stage. This prevents me from feeling disappointed when my name is not called.

Hat draws can also lead to a bit of a roller coaster in terms of the quality of the stories or content included. Since the acts are not vetted in advance, there is as good a chance that the story you are hearing is unpolished or unclear. This is the spin-the-wheel-of-fortune chance you take as an audience member for these kinds of shows. On the other hand, by setting limits such as a five to six-minute time limit, you might get three minutes into the story before you realize it's falling off the rails and can rest assured that it will at least be over in a few minutes.

I love one of *The Moth StorySLAM* traditions—inviting the storytellers (who want to) who were not selected for the ten spots designated in the evening to come up and tell the "first line" of their story to the audience. In Berkeley, we sometimes get twenty-eight or more entries for ten spots, so having those extra eighteen people up on stage telling a small slice of the story they would have told gives us a wonderful closing taste of the variety of life experiences sitting all around us throughout the event. It affirms what the show generally suggests—we *all* have stories in us, and so many of them are so interesting! Inviting the "remainders" to the stage also honors their patience and willingness to participate, letting them have a moment, even if truncated, to share a bit of themselves with the room.

Curated

Shows that are not hat draw/open mic formats are generally considered "curated" shows. For these kinds of shows, there are a few common varieties and considerations.

Repertory Companies

Some curated shows rely on a set or rotating cast of players, storytellers, or performers. These shows are typically closed to outside storytellers, unless invited in as guest performers. Repertory companies might include scripted or unscripted acts, relying on a certain brand-consistency for their audience.

To be included in a repertory company show, you may need to audition or be invited to be a member of the company. Alternately, you may introduce yourself to the company or director/producer/cast to indicate your interest in performing with them in a future show and wait to be invited or included.

Producer-Curated

A common format for a curated show or showcase is for a producer or production group to invite performers for their events. Many times, the producers of these shows will look for a specific kind of voice, variety, or tone of story to build an event's entertainment.

Alternately, when considering the marketing and promotion of their own shows, producers may look to include acts or performers that would be considered a "draw" for their audience—someone with credits or a following of their own that might lead to interest or ticket sales for the show.

To be included in a producer-curated show, it's best first to attend the show or to reach out to the show producer with an inquiry about how the show is booked. Learning their selection process will give you a road map to follow to get more stage time and practice for your own storytelling.

Hybrid/Specialty Shows

Some curated shows are in fact hybrid shows, incorporating some hat-draw components in their lineup. B Frayn Masters' Portland based Backfence PDX series used to invite storytellers in a curated format, while leaving a spot in the lineup for three or four audience volunteers to come up and share a one-minute story with the audience on the same theme.

Their current show, Backfence PDX: Russian Roulette, is a super fun, high stakes format, where six experienced storytellers spin a wheel full of juicy story prompts and, with only five minutes to prepare, must come up with a true five-minute story to tell, live, based on that word. The audience votes for a winner at the end of the night who receives prizes and money.

StorySLAM Oakland similarly invites (and pays!) a few "featured" storytellers and supplements the rest of the show with hat draw attendees. This kind of hybrid can work very well for smaller community-oriented events. There's always guaranteed to be a few "ringers" with prepared stories and the nice organized chaos of the hat draw to include the community. As these kinds of events grow, the storytelling tends to get better and better and the options for the host to "discover" new "featured" storytellers grows as well.

If you are considering hosting an event like this, it's highly advisable to collect storyteller information (phone, email, etc.) to contact them later...and if you have plans to record or otherwise use the stories, they tell to promote your own show (including photographs), make sure to provide a "release" of some kind that grants you that permission.

The current standard for such paperwork is to grant the producer the rights to use your story in their podcasts or other productions, but not giving them any rights to the intellectual property itself. In other words, it's still your story and your content. They are only given access to the specific performance you are giving on that day.

Here is an example contract. Feel free to modify this for your own use. (Disclaimer: I am not a lawyer. That you copied this out of a book does not mean it will necessarily protect you. Seek more professional advice.):

Storytelling Show Release Form

Thank you for participating in _____ (show name). Please fill in and sign this form to give us permission to use the images, photographs, documents, written materials, voice and sound recordings, and any other materials you have provided to go with your story.

Participant's Name:_____

Project Title: _____

Producer: _____ Date: _____

I agree that my voice recordings and the images submitted and taken during the project as well as my or my organization's writings, documents, and photographs may be distributed by agents, employees, or representatives of _____ without limitation through presentations, exhibition, website, book, and internet publishing. I understand that I am granting all rights to these documents and images without compensation to _____ for educational, noncommercial use. I hereby hold harmless and release and forever discharge the producers from all claims, demands, and causes of action which I, my heirs, representatives, executors, administrators, or any other persons acting on my behalf or on behalf of my estate have or may have by reason of this authorization.

Date: _____ By: _____

Phone: _____ Print Name: _____

Email: _____ Phone: _____

The Moth Main Stage format often mixes up its selection process—"discovering" storytellers through its StorySLAM shows, inviting authors or celebrities, and even taking submissions via a telephone hotline. For those shows, the performers are directed and coached by a director who advises the storyteller in ways to help shape and perform their stories for the best overall impact and effect.

Regardless of the format, it's always advisable to research or attend the show you are interested in before you put your name in to perform there—listen to their podcast, watch their YouTube videos, or show up at a performance. Do this, especially if you are not sure if your story or style will blend with the show.

Playing to an Audience

You've made it. You're at the show. You're on stage. What do you do? Here are some ideas, tips, and exercises you can employ and practice for performance to an audience.

Warm-Up

Though storytelling may not seem like "acting," these helpful exercises and routines often performed by thespians before going on stage that are not unlike the stretches and warm-ups done by athletes before a game or a strenuous workout. Your voice and body can benefit from some simple warm-up exercises such as:

Physical Warm-Ups

It is hard to feel fully present and "in your body" if you have not moved, stretched, or activated your body. These are some easy-to-do physical warm-ups, some of which can even be done while sitting in the audience at a storytelling show while watching the other performers!

- Basic stretching of your arms, shoulders, legs, and neck
- Stretch the muscles of your face by making large and small exaggerated expressions
- Mouth muscle massage, using your fingers to lightly rub your jaw and cheeks
- Run tongue along gum line, all the way around the mouth
- March, lifting your knees and arms high, for thirty-three steps in place

Breathing

Breathing is an excellent warm-up exercise for storytelling. The breath helps you relax as well as affect the tone and quality of your voice.

- Inhale for a count of 4 and exhale through motorboat lips for a count of 8

- Then inhale for a count of 4 and motorboat exhale for a count of 12

- Then inhale for a count of 4 and motorboat exhale for a count of 16

- Then inhale for a count of 4 and motorboat exhale for a count of 20

Vocal Warm-Ups

Like your body and your breath, it's important and helpful to activate your voice by doing vocal warmups like the following:

On your way to the venue, sing along with the radio or a song you like

Humming and chewing with lips closed

Slowly repeat a few tongue twisters to warm up the mouth muscles like:

"Red Leather Yellow Leather. Lips Teeth Tip of the Tongue."

"Good Blood Bad Blood."

"She stood on the balcony, inexplicably mimicking him hiccupping, while amicably welcoming him home."

Sing arpeggios—up and down the scale to loosen your vocal muscles

Vocal Exercise (1, 1-2-1, …)

BATS Improv in San Francisco is one of the pre-eminent improv theaters in the world. Music Director and Improv Musician J. Raoul Brody leads the following vocal (singing) warm-up to increase the blood flow to the muscles around your mouth and throat.

Sing 1, 1-2-1, 1-2-3-2-1…with the pitch of each "number" going up and down the major scale:

1-2-3-4-3-2-1
1-2-3-4-5-4-3-2-1
1-2-3-4-5-6-5-4-3-2-1
1-2-3-4-5-6-7-6-5-4-3-2-1
1-2-3-4-5-6-7-8-7-6-5-4-3-2-1

Then do it in reverse, singing down, then up the scale for each number:

8
8-7-8
8-7-6-7-8
8-7-6-5-6-7-8
8-7-6-5-4-5-6-7-8
8-7-6-5-4-3-4-5-6-7-8
8-7-6-5-4-3-2-3-4-5-6-7-8
8-7-6-5-4-3-2-1-2-3-4-5-6-7-8

Microphones

Most, though not all, shows will provide a microphone for
the storytellers. Some shows request the performers keep the

microphone in a stationary position while others are alright with handholding the mic.

Stationary Microphone

I recommend keeping the microphone in place for most true storytelling. This allows you the maximum freedom to use your hands, arms, and body in the telling of your story.

Step right up to the microphone, leaving about three fingers' distance between your mouth and the mic. This is not rap music or stand up where you'd want to put your mouth right up against the microphone!

Angle the microphone so that it points up at a slight angle toward your chin. When you speak into it, you should be speaking "across" the microphone more than directly "into" it. This will limit the amount of "popping" that occurs when you speak sibilant consonants like P and K and T.

Do not be afraid of the microphone! Many novice performers think of the microphone as an obstacle between themselves and the audience and inadvertently speak around, behind, or away from it. This is very frustrating for the audience, who can see you speak but will have trouble hearing you. Step right up and speak into the microphone.

If you have physical activity or motion that pulls you away from the microphone, make your motion and then finish the words into the microphone, not while you are lying on the ground or flailing beside it.

If you have a wide range of volume in your story, it's a good idea to practice with the mic—getting a little closer for the quiet moments and farther for the louder yelled or screamed parts.

Handheld Microphone

The handheld microphone style seen by hosts, singers, stand-ups, and storytellers takes practice to perfect. It frees you to move around the stage, but limits you in other ways, by taking one hand out of play.

As with a stationary mic, you must modulate the distance the mic is from your own mouth—keeping it about three fingers' distance away, for less distortion and best vocal quality.

I caution the inexperienced for this main reason—commanding the microphone in your hand is a skill in itself. Without a plan or confidence, people holding the microphone tend to wander or pace back and forth. This is why I prefer to and generally advise planting the mic, and yourself, to tell your story.

Headset Microphone

If, for whatever reason, you are asked to or choose to, a headset microphone is the closest you will get in a performance to a freestyle, hands-free storytelling experience that can be heard by an audience.

Generally, these are worn around your ear with a small mic that lives close to your mouth and a wire that runs to a pack that transmits the sound to a speaker.

Aside from the "pacing" or wandering issue, a wireless mic is a nice option as it appears the most natural to the audience. You can simply tell the story without any kind of tether in your hand or on the stage.

The only thing to watch out for with a headset is the placement of the microphone. If it wanders too far from the speaker's mouth, it may be hard to hear. For this reason, some performers use medical (transparent) tape on their face to keep the mic close to the mouth. If the tape looks too shiny in the light you can use (no joke) Monistat cream to dull it (pro tip).

Body Language

How you hold your body and your presence on stage makes an impact on how the audience receives your story. Something I enjoy observing with storytellers is their natural body language, posture, and presence. As the nature of this kind of performance is personal, it's not essential to change your behavior if what you are doing conveys your natural way of talking, gesturing, or being!

On the other hand, I find it helpful to be aware of how certain behaviors or instincts are perceived from the outside—and to know that it's possible to modify the impression I am giving off based on conscious decisions I make with regards to my body and overall stage presence.

I think a performance is and should be as individual as the person giving it. I don't recommend adopting some kind of behaviors to project a false version of yourself, for fear that it will read as inauthentic and lose credibility with the audience. Better for you to come off as awkward and nervous, if that's how you are feeling, than to feel awkward and nervous and to overcompensate with a false bravado.

We can read through such false behaviors and may, in fact, disbelieve other parts of you or your story if you come off as insincere. So, proceed with caution, but consider the following:

Eye Contact

As in one-on-one interactions, eye contact can be a powerful kind of body language on stage. In brightly lit theatrical lighting, you may have no eye contact whatsoever with the audience.

For one unaccustomed to this kind of lighting, it's helpful to get a sense of the environment before taking the stage. Since you will have no interaction with the audience, you may want to set your "gaze" somewhere along the horizon or back of the theater. This will give the overall impression that you are looking "out" as you tell your story.

For other lighting environments, you are likely able to see the audience. In this case, I enjoy using a "system" where I deliver a part of my story focused in one area of the audience. As I complete a sentence or a thought, I move my attention to another person, area, or section of the theater. In this way, I don't appear to be fixed in one specific direction, as if I am addressing the entire theater while still making each area feel like they're getting some "personal" attention.

A caution if using a system like this—don't act like a "sprinkler" and rotate back and forth as you speak. Doing this looks highly unnatural. You would not do this if addressing a room full of friends, so don't do it when telling a story.

Eye contact, or the impression/illusion of eye contact when addressing a large group of people, personalizes the performer, giving me the sense that you are telling *me* a story.

Occasionally, to ground a story in the "now," I find it helpful to look for a face in the crowd that is buying what I'm selling. Someone who is smiling, nodding, actively listening. I will talk to *them* for a phrase or an idea. And if I'm feeling it, I may even talk right *to* them. It's a way to make the entire experience feel a lot more intimate when any individual may be singled out or talked to. I find it can even make the rest of the audience perk up, as it feels spontaneous and present instead of a pre-planned or canned interaction.

Breath Control

It wasn't until I heard myself recorded that I started appreciating the importance of breathing *while* telling my stories. I'm telling a story and every so often I make a smacking sound with my tongue and upper palate. While not clearly connected, I now listen to myself while I'm speaking. When I feel myself short of breath or making sounds like this, it's a cue to me to breathe.

Breathing while you tell your story is actually an important flavor to inject into the performance itself. It grounds the storyteller, it slows or moderates the pace that you are setting, and it nourishes your brain as you make your way into and through the story.

The alternative is, generally, a sense that the storyteller is out of control, rushing through the beats or details of the story to get through it. I understand the impulse to do this for timed shows—"I only have five minutes!" But isn't it preferable to hear a *good* five-minute story than to hear a seven-minute story rushed into a five-minute window?

If I have to tell a five-minute story, I'd much rather slow it down and omit a scene, beat, or detail in the story, rather than sacrificing my control as a storyteller to the experience the audience is receiving when they hear it.

In the same spirit, when I feel the audience is not quite with me as I am telling a story, I sometimes feel an instinct to rush through it to the "good part" just ahead. But to the contrary, if I've lost them or if I haven't yet "won" them, I've had better success at getting there by slowing down, by breathing and recentering myself into the story I am telling, to why I think this is a story worth telling in the first place.

Reading the Room

A final pointer and tip for storytelling shows: all rooms are different, and it's highly advised to take stock of that and "read the room" before your performance. Is this the kind of story that is appropriate to tell here? Is there something better to try or to tell because of where I am or who is in attendance?

Recently, my company at BATS Improv, under the direction of Lisa Rowland, put on a month of shows we called *The Gather*, where storytellers telling true life stories were paired with improvisors who took the story content as their initiation material to launch into scenes that explored their themes, relationships, characters, or overall subject matter.

We invited a wide range of storytellers with diverse life experiences— not just comic ones—to get as diverse as possible a pool of topics to explore on stage. This was not "bar-prov" improvisation with proctologist jokes or scatological humor; the push here was for real people telling real stories to drive real scenes that could build on or even deepen our connection to the storytellers, and hence to ourselves.

The storytellers were all very intrigued by the concept of seeing how the improvisors would take their stories and "play" with them. Some told lighter stories: Milton Schuyler related his story about painting the large living room in Mill Valley. Others told heavier ones: A storyteller named 3858 talked about his crack addiction prior to his jail sentence.

For all, I noticed and admired the way they read the room, each taking stock of the setting, the audience, and the makeup of the improvisor cast, and making their own judgment calls for what kinds of stories they would tell on that stage. I considered it a sign that they were feeling comfortable and confident when they would go for a deeper, more powerful memory.

Still others, like storyteller Greg Quiroga, changed their stories from what they'd planned to tell in reaction to the other stories they were hearing that night. Several serious, painful, or touching stories in a row could be great or they could create a heavy, weighted experience for the audience, one which Greg determined he could help to shift by telling one of his lighter or more comic stories.

In contrast, I've seen storytellers arrive on stage at *The Moth* StorySLAM that came off as very unprepared and unprofessional— eating food as they told their stories, or delivering wandering, aimless narratives without a real story or point. By not reading the room, you can inadvertently have a negative effect on the show as a whole.

Producing Your Own Shows

Here are some basics and ideas for producing your own storytelling shows, should you want to take control of your own destiny and create opportunities for yourself and your community.

Supplies

It doesn't take much to put on a storytelling show. You only really need:

- Somewhere to do it

- People to tell stories

The larger the event, the more involved the preparations would need to be, of course. A gathering of friends to tell stories at a public park wouldn't need microphones, publicity, lighting, and the like.

Venue Ideas

- Public Spaces, Community Centers, Libraries

- Bars, Restaurants, Cafes

- Theaters, Schools, Colleges, Religious Buildings

- Art Galleries, Gymnasiums, Hospitals

When I am looking to put on a show, I like to visit a number of venue options, starting with ones I already have a connection with such as a theater, a café I am a regular patron of, or a space where I have seen a similar kind of event.

Depending on the place, there could be no cost for the use of the space (as you may be bringing in customers), or there may be fees to rent, use, and clean the space and staff the show.

On the larger scale, when I have rented a black box theater to put on a show, I've needed a few more elements for the event:

- House Manager to sell/collect tickets

- Lighting and/or Sound Board Operator to manage the tech during the show

- Stage Manager for larger productions to manage the flow of who is on/off stage

- Photo, Sound, and/or Video Engineers to capture and process the show for posterity

- Paid or volunteer assistants for ushering, cleaning, or otherwise assisting in the smooth running of the event

What's nice about this format is that it is very scalable, from the smallest and most intimate living room to the largest stage or screen you can imagine.

Logistics

A number of years ago, I put on a show called *The A**hole Monologues.* The show was a fundraiser for Crohn's and Colitis, two inflammatory diseases that affect close family and friends of mine. The title was a cheeky (forgive the pun) play on Eve Ensler's wonderful *Vagina Monologues,* with the performers invited to craft short variety-style pieces revolving around the theme of "A**holes" (any definition).

My first production was held at the Bayfront Theater in San Francisco, at ten thirty on a Friday night, as the "late night" show following an eight to ten o'clock show in the same space.

Casting was a blend of me asking people I knew for interest in taking part. I also put out a "call for submissions" on internet bulletin boards like Craigslist and received submitted scripts, resumes, and links to see their work.

In a short time, I had enough participants to put a fairly large show together. There was a rental fee for the two-hundred-seat theater, and additional costs for:

- Posters printed to advertise the event around town

- A website put up to promote the show

- Matching stools purchased at IKEA to have a clean, consistent look on stage

- Food to keep backstage in the green room for the performers

- Food and drinks for an after party I organized as thanks for the performers

I met with all the performers at least once to see their act and, if needed, gave some guidance or feedback that would help it to integrate well into the show. This often involved cuts in material to help it fit the limited time slots allocated.

When the show approached, my time was divided between multiple areas:

- Communicating with the venue and performers so all knew what was happening and when

- Promoting the show via email, advertising on "events" boards, and hanging posters

- Selling advance tickets through a website that allows, for a small fee, tickets to be sold for any event

On the night of the show, designate a call time when the performers and staff should show up in advance of the show. In this time, you can situate the performers to know where and what to do. For an open mic or hat draw type event, this would include collecting the participant names and distributing any paperwork you may want them to fill out.

Having a host to move the show along is optional. Some shows, like *The A**hole Monologues*, had a pre-set run order, so we did not need a host to introduce their acts; they simply took their cues to enter as the previous act was ending. Other storytelling shows, like *The Moth*, use a host to smooth the transitions in between.

Shape of Show

To me, the key to a successful or unsuccessful event is what we call the "shape of show." Shape of show is a shorthand way to indicate the importance of seeing the entire show, or event, as more than the sum of its parts. It's not just a collection of stories—it's an event unto itself, with a beginning, middle and end.

The shape of show, then, is the rise and fall, the humor and pathos, the pacing of the experience for the audience and performers alike. Shape of show, for example, can be a determining factor if you are setting a time limit (or not) for your performers. If one story lasts five minutes, followed by one that lasts fourteen minutes, followed by one that lasts thirty minutes…the audience may be confused. Calibrating their expectations for whether they are watching a longer piece or a shorter one sets their own internal rhythm for the show you are putting out there.

When I am hosting an open mic show, I have no control over the content being told on the stage, but I do have the power, as host, to shift the feeling in the theater between acts. A general rule of thumb I try to employ is this—when the show is going well, get out of its way. In other words, when the stories are good and the audience is having a good time, I do not try to "make it about me" as the host and draw attention to myself. It's more like a great rally in tennis—I want to keep it going and not mess it up.

On the other hand, when a story goes a little sideways and the audience seems disconnected, confused, or otherwise off-kilter, I feel it's my job as the host to right the ship—to win them back with interstitial business that brings them back to the experience of being here, now, together.

Here is an example. A few years ago, tensions were high across the country with high profile incidents involving police shootings of

African Americans. Black Lives Matter was gaining momentum and rallies were being held nationwide to protest senseless killings and incidents filling the headlines.

On the night of one of these incidents in 2015, Freddie Gray was injured and ultimately died while in police custody in Baltimore. Widespread nationwide protests were held that day. That evening, I was hosting a show in San Francisco on the theme of "Confusion." The theme had been set long before the trouble in the news, but the feeling in the theater was tense and charged.

During my warm-up of the audience, usually a relatively lighthearted affair, someone from the audience yelled out about Baltimore, that we acknowledge what was happening. Sometimes, all that's needed is for the audience to have their feelings acknowledged. There may have been little that we could do in this little theater, at this time, but acknowledging the protests and the difficult things we were processing in our country helped to diffuse some of that tension, as did acknowledging the fact that, in some way, by telling our stories to each other, we were in fact making the world a more connected place at a time when people were feeling disconnected from each other.

About halfway through the show, a storyteller was picked from the hat that I'd never met before. Her name is Suzanne Barakat, and her story was about how her brother, his wife, and her sister were murdered in an act of racial violence in their home. It was as powerful a story as I'd maybe ever heard on that stage. Deeply affecting, this woman opened her heart to share her pain at this tragic, senseless loss.

Now, StorySLAMs are a grab bag of performers. The host's role in all of this is to preserve or smooth the shape of the show. So, what could I do after this story? Half of me wanted to end the show right then and there. But the other half knew I had a job to do, and a responsibility to keep the show moving. To make a joke would be disrespectful to Suzanne's story and the power it held on all of us. So, I turned it back over to the audience in that moment. "Turn to someone near you and give them a hug." The room erupted in love, strangers hugging strangers, releasing their emotions and actually connecting with each other after hearing the saddest story imaginable.

It was a powerful moment and a memorable one. Then, another storyteller was called up. The host's role in this is to smooth the waters. You don't want the next storyteller to feel at a disadvantage, that they're walking into a no-win situation. You want the audience to be as warm and receptive to each performer as possible. By releasing the emotion of Suzanne's story, the next storyteller could take her own deep breath and start anew.

This was an example of where you can use the energy of what's already happening, in the room and all around you, to reframe and preserve the shape of the show.

In another case, I was able to use improvisation to save a show from near disaster.

It is the first ever GrandSLAM held in San Francisco. Ten storytellers who have won individual StorySLAMs are squaring off, telling their stories to a capacity crowd of 1,400 people at the Castro Theater in San Francisco. I am hosting the show, facing the biggest crowd I have ever performed for in my life.

My main job when hosting *The Moth* is to keep the flow of the show moving. To warm up the stage and the crowd to be good, engaged listeners. And to involve the audience by reading their submitted "slips," paper strips on which they can anonymously participate. I also collect the scores from audience-volunteer judges.

We are just past the halfway mark of the show and have welcomed the crowd back from their intermission break. The entire audience is in their seats preparing to hear the sixth (of ten) storyteller of the night. Just then, the sound goes completely out. Silence. Nothing.

I am standing center stage in a theater with 1,400 people, including the executive directing staff from *The Moth*'s New York headquarters, staring at me while technicians frantically debug the problem and try to figure out what was happening.

While I am trained as and perform as an improvisor, I am very fortunate in that case to have my wife in the front row of that theater. She too is an improvisor and, with as cool a look as I've maybe ever seen her give me, she said two words that changed the entire night, "sound effects."

"Sound effects" is the name of an audience participation improv game. In it, the performer or performers on stage do a scene, usually with a large amount of mimed "space object" work—using props, opening and closing doors, things like that. When played as a game, the audience is directed to provide, in unison, all the sound effects for the scene. This is a game I have played plenty of times in small improv shows. I had no idea how 1,400 people were going to spontaneously work together in creating the sound effects for a scene.

But I was game to try. In as loud a stage voice as I could, without the benefit of a microphone, I explained, "I'm going to do a scene, and you are going to do all the sound effects, ok?" "Ok!" I heard back. I was off and running. Walking, actually. As I walked to the left side of the stage, I heard the audience STOMPING THEIR FEET, making the sound of my feet walking!

I reached my arms forward and, with a recognizable gesture, mimed turning on a faucet and washing my hands. "SHHHHHHHHHHHHHHHHHHHH," the 1,400-person crowd provided, filling the two-leveled theater with incredible surround sound of my simple actions.

I turned off the faucet and walked to the right. STOMP STOMP STOMP STOMP. I stopped center stage and mimed mounting a motorcycle. Lifting up and down the crowd knew just what to do, "VROOOOOOOM"

For three or four minutes, I held the audience's focus and attention with this diversionary game until I got the nod from the sound team. The mics were working again.

I introduced the next storyteller and took my seat. It wasn't until I sat down that the sweat started to pour from my head. My heart racing now that I was out of the spotlight, I had a moment to reflect on what had just happened. How crazy it was to successfully hold the attention of the audience with, literally, nothing. No sounds. No props. Just a game. I held the shape of the show and moved it along in a way that I will never forget.

And I think anyone can do it. Stay present in the moment with what is happening on the stage, in the room, and in your community. The more present you seem, the more connected the audience will stay with you and with the show you are putting on.

Run Order

Unless you are hosting an open format slam-style show, you will usually want to craft a run order for the performance. I've produced many shows, balancing a wide variety of acts and storytelling styles.

For one run of *The A**hole Monologues,* I had to balance musical comedy with deadpan spoken word performance art. A multi-media slide show with a painful tale of living with Crohn's disease. It was a crazy mishmash of acts that, aside from all being connected to the word, "a**hole," had nothing else in common.

I discovered through these productions valuable lessons about how to craft such shows. While each individual act or story will take the audience on a "journey" of some kind, perhaps emotional or intellectual, each act on its own will take on a kind of presence that is represented in your show. Some stories start neutral and end sad. Some start down and end with screaming and high energy. Some start with mystery and end with humor. The key for plotting these acts in a show is those beats—beginning and end—to determine their place in the run order of the show.

For example, I like to start a storytelling showcase with a generally relatable, often lighthearted humorous story. This warms the audience up to the act of listening to stories and engages and entertains them. Leaving that story on a "high" is then a good place to either "ride the wave" and move into another "high energy" or similarly toned story.

This creates a pattern and a feeling of happiness, curiosity, or engagement for the audience. With this trust established by the first two stories, I can then throw a curveball. Shift the energy with a strange story, a darker story, or anything else that might be a "standalone" kind of tale. Once that is in the mix, the audience's expectation spectrum has widened. They have seen a pattern, then the pattern is broken. This opens a curiosity channel—what will I hear next?

Another consideration I make, related to the beats of a story's start and end, is to pair them that way.

- Story one starts neutral and ends high
- Story two starts high and ends sweet
- Story three starts sweet and ends angry
- Story four starts intense and ends funny
- Story five starts funny and ends explosively funny

Gradually, you carry the audience on a journey from start of the show to end. As the material will vary, I tend to walk the audience "down the stairway" into deeper, more profound, or more personal territory later into the show.

For a ten-story evening, if I had my choice, I would put the most serious, or impactful, story close to, but not at the end. Perhaps seventh, eighth, or ninth out of the ten stories. This carries the audience on a roller coaster, from high, feel-good stories, deeper into more serious or touching stories, and then back up to a high conclusion.

In the end, the feeling I like to have when I leave a show is that I myself have been changed in some way through the stories. Ira Glass, in his show, *Seven Things I Learned,* compares the way he structures the shape of his radio show, *This American Life,* in a similar way:

"*Fiddler on the Roof...*starts out as a comedy about a guy trying to marry off his three daughters," Glass said. "The plot gets increasingly serious throughout the course of it as each girl chooses a boy who is less and less acceptable to the parents."

The narrative movement of the play, from comedy to tragedy, is Glass's template for *This American Life.* The movement from a personal story to "a bigger human something" as Glass put it—is another way in which *Fiddler* influences *This American Life.*

Any show can adopt this methodology, moving the arc of the stories from small, personal, and comedic to increasingly serious, personal, and poignant. A motif I also adopt in planning the run of a show is to preface a "lift" before a "drop." Like a roller coaster raising us up, humor, fun, or action can open us up for a descent into a more weighty or meaningful story.

With that strategy in mind, this was the end sequence of one run of *The A**hole Monologues:*

- M.I. Blue: "Sound Poem"

  – A build from quiet to screaming-loud story about a
    man's sex life.

- Mark Growden: "The Nasty"

  – A minor-key waltz played live on an accordion by a
    tattooed troubadour about missing "doing the nasty"
    with his lover while on a screen behind him, we watch a
    slideshow of his relationship with a blow-up doll.

- Jennifer Castle: "Crohn's"

  – A short, poignant, recounting of life with Crohn's Disease.
    It goes deep into the pain and embarrassment of this
    incurable condition, and then ends on an uplifting note of
    optimism and hope.

- Daniel Weiss: "Do Not Enter (The Song of my A**hole)"

  – A melodic show tune about setting limits for one's
    own body, which builds into an oom-pa-pa-style song
    involving the entire company.

Balance the flow of the show and nearly any act can find a place, so
long as it fits the overall balance of the rest of the program. Overly
long content rarely integrates, unless it is the featured act of the event.
Very short content, by contrast, can itself help to lift the audience,
especially after a weaker or lower-energy story. That kind of variety—
with very short-form content—can be very unexpected and delight
the audience who was expecting a longer story or scene.

Online Storytelling Show

In the midst of the global lockdown stemming from the coronavirus pandemic, artists and performers of all kinds pivoted from live performance to innovative and exciting uses of internet technologies to perform and stay connected with audiences worldwide. The unexpected limitation of "social distancing," where performers could not be co-located, became an excellent example of the Improvisor Mindset in action—using what is right in front of you, dealing with the unexpected, and adapting to the current situation.

Conference Software

Software like Skype, Zoom, Google Chat, and FaceTime, while intended for group meetings and conferences, can work remarkably well to unite distant performers and broadcast them around the world. Zoom's ability to switch between a "gallery mode" that shows all the performers at once and "speaker view" to feature just one performer at a time allows for a nice theatrical feeling, similar to a storytelling show.

> Pro Tip: Zoom allows for a video setting to "hide non-video participants." In gallery mode, anyone with their camera off can still be heard but not seen, and the visible parties' screens enlarge to fill the space. So, one camera on allows for a solo story. Two becomes a dialogue between those two.

Without too much trouble, these sessions can also be live streamed on platforms including YouTube Live, Facebook Live, and Twitch.tv to an audience around the world! In some cases, passwords are used for ticket-buyers to access the stream. In others, the performers put work out for free and ask for donations from viewers.

The exciting aspect of this to me is how even when people cannot physically be in the same space, the tools and technologies that we have access to can be repurposed for artistic expression and connection, something storytelling does so well.

One challenge with performing in this way is the silence of performing without a live audience. There is no laughter or audible audience response when you are telling a story alone in your dining room! Another feature of conferencing software that allows for interactivity is the "chat" function, where, though they cannot be heard, the audience can participate or encourage the storyteller or performer with their words.

Chapter 12

Storytelling Resources

Armed with information and just enough confidence to be dangerous, it is time to put your storytelling to work. Apply this sequence and process every time you have a story to tell:

1. Ideate. Flesh out the contents of your imagination.

2. Develop your stories without attachment to outcome. Don't be protective about the direction you intended for the story as you discover what the story wants to be.

3. Experiment with different structural styles to find what suits the story best.

4. Tell your story to a friend, a class, or at a show.

5. Modify the story based on your feelings and the reactions of others.

6. Repeat.

"If you want to be a killer storyteller, then one of the best things you can do for yourself is absorb good stories."

—KEVIN ALLISON, HOST OF *RISK!*

Here are some additional resources that can be accessed for up-to-date information and entertainment on the subject of storytelling. Since storytelling transcends genre, these lists are a mix of types and styles of show.

Podcasts

- *The Moth*

  - Each podcast episode, also known as *The Moth Radio Hour*, is a collection of around five stories bundled around a theme.

- *This American Life*

  - Ira Glass hosts this storytelling program that set the bar for all the other programs around, delving deeply into stories from around the world.

- *Snap Judgment*

  - Glynn Washington's captivating podcast and radio show features true storytellers with underscores soundtracks, making the listening experience more cinematic and exciting.

- *RISK!*

  - Kevin Allison curates this collection of stories told by comics, actors, writers, and entertainers of all kinds. Each episode has a loose theme. They usually skew scary, dangerous, and life transforming, often with a dark edge.

- *Ear Hustle*

  - *Ear Hustle* invites prison inmates to tell their stories from behind bars. Episodes offer an unfiltered look at life behind bars.

Live Shows

Nearly every city now features opportunities to listen to, and to tell, live stories. Most cities have their own local flavor and spin. Here are a few kinds and brands you may look for in your local area:

- *The Moth*—www.themoth.org

  - StorySLAMs are held in twenty cities around the world every month.

  - Main Stage shows are held periodically, featuring longer format curated stories.

  - GrandSLAMs are held wherever StorySLAMs are, but less often.

- *Snap Judgment*—www.snapjudgment.org

  - *Snap Judgment* tapes live shows around the country and receives submissions via their website.

- *RISK!*—www.Risk-show.com

  - Live show that is taped for podcast and hosted by Kevin Allison.

Books

- *Story* by Robert McKee

  - An excellent resource for screenwriting, including breakdowns of beats, scenes, sequences, and acts for long form storytelling.

- *The Hero with a Thousand Faces* by Joseph Campbell

  - The original and most-often cited resource for comparative mythology and the Hero's Journey monomyth structure.

- *The Writer's Journey* by Christopher Vogler

  - An application of the Hero's Journey to screenwriting, with ample examples of where and how the Joseph Campbell mythic structure is used in modern filmmaking.

- *Made to Stick* by Dan Heath and Chip Heath

  - A spectacular read, about how some ideas last and others die. Applied to storytelling, their "SUCCESS" formula is a great gauge for strengthening any story.

- *Devotional Cinema* by Nathaniel Dorsky

  - Powerful transcription of Dorsky's academic lecture, about the power the form of a story can have on how it is received.

- *How to Write Your Best Story* by Phillip Martin

Websites

- TheMoth.org

  - Resources, stories, and information about live events.

- plotdevices.co/pages/how-to-use-the-storyclock-notebook

- Resource for structuring and planning any story using a "clock" model.

- www.duarte.com/presentation-skills-resources

  - Nancy Duarte, a leading voice on Brand Storytelling, has a helpful blog.

- storycenter.org/blog

  - Stories and resources for storytellers.

- www.getstoried.com

  - Michael Margolis' site filled with free resources for storytelling.

- www.improvgames.com

  - William Hall's (cofounder of BATS Improv) resource site for theater and improv games, including instructional videos for how to play.

Communities

- National Storytelling Network (NSN)

  - NSN is a professional organization that helps to organize resources for tellers and festival planners.

- International Storytelling Center (ISC)

  - The ISC runs the National Storytelling Festival in Jonesborough, TN.

Afterword

I sincerely hope you found this book to be enjoyable and helpful on your own journey with story, storytelling, creativity, improvisation, or any other pursuits. This is my first published book, and in the story spine of my own life, every day I continue to learn and welcome new experiences. I welcome your feedback, ideas for inclusion in follow-up books, and of course, hearing your stories! Please visit my website at www.coreyrosen.com, and my Facebook and Instagram pages (fb.me/StoryRosen & instagram.com/storyrosen) where I will be listing additional resources, lessons, and of course STORIES and opportunities where you can see, hear, and tell your own.

Please send any other feedback (Yes, and!) my way directly! If you like the book, please email storytelling@coreyrosen.com, share it with someone you think would enjoy it, and POST A REVIEW on Amazon!

Thank you for reading!

Acknowledgments

I am deeply grateful for everyone who helped make this book possible: The Rosen family with special thanks to Jerry & Maxine. My editor Brenda Knight and everyone at Mango Publishing. Randy Peyser who made it happen. The friends and colleagues who so dearly shared their time, energy, ideas, and stories with me, including Steven Rosen, Adam Rosen, Mitch Temple, Leila Chesloff, Jeff Hanson, Lara Nuer, Milton Schuyler, Eva Schlesinger, Randy Beard, Dave Mahony, and Ted & Marian Zachary. The theaters and communities where I have shared, listened to, and learned storytelling including and especially *The Moth*, *BATS Improv, Tippett Studio*, and *The Writing Pad*. Extra special thanks with sugar on top to Noli, Henry, and Jenny Rosen, my home team who are a part of every story I have ever told and will ever tell.

Index

About the Author

Corey Rosen—photo by Stu Maschwitz

Corey Rosen is a writer, actor, visual effects producer, and storytelling teacher based in San Francisco, California. He hosts *The Moth* StorySLAMs and GrandSLAMs and won their first ever Bay Area StorySLAM (2012). He has been featured on *The Moth Radio Hour*. He is a regular contributor and on-air personality for Alice Radio's *The Sarah and Vinnie Show*. Corey is a company performer at BATS Improv, one of the world's foremost centers for improvisational theater. Corey got his start writing for Comedy Central and Jim Henson Productions. As staff writer for Lucasfilm Animation and Tippett Studio, he wrote the screenplays for films and theme park rides and attractions exhibiting around the world. When not writing,

Corey works as a visual effects artist and creative director. He has credits on dozens of movies, including several Star Wars films and Disney's *A Christmas Carol.* He has taught in the MFA Animation program at Academy of Art University and for the Writing Pad. He has written and directed television commercials and award-winning short films. He lives in San Francisco with his wife Jenny and two story-inspiring children. www.coreyrosen.com.